"An excellent and much needed tale c from hyper-schooling. In *At What Cost? Defending Adolescent Development in Fiercely Competitive Schools*, veteran psychologist David Gleason exposes the problems, explains the causes and provides sound suggestions for parents, educators and school leaders."

Yong Zhao, Ph.D. Presidential Chair, Director, Institute of Global and Online Education; Professor, Department of Educational Methodology, Policy and Leadership, College of Education, University of Oregon

"We are experiencing an epidemic of anxiety in children and teens and our 'finest' schools are part of the problem. Yet as David Gleason argues, these schools can also be essential to the solution. In his new book *At What Cost? Defending Adolescent Development in Fiercely Competitive Schools*, Gleason makes a passionate plea to educators and parents alike to ratchet down the pressure on teens. Gleason's research reveals the bind that educators and parents are in, and introduces important ways that schools and parents can ease back and change. Attention must be paid."

Michael Thompson, Ph.D., International Speaker, Author of *The Pressured Child: Helping Your Child Find Success in School and Life*

"Drawing from Gleason's more than 20 years as a clinical psychologist—and grounded in rich, practical, and heartfelt examples—*At What Cost? Defending Adolescent Development in Fiercely Competitive Schools* makes a compelling case for bringing the powerful principles of *Immunity to Change* coaching to the world of high performance schools. A guide for parents and educators striving to better understand the "double bind" driving mounting academic pressures and competition, this book offers a hopeful and promising pathway to a better future for all. It is a gift and a must read for all who care for our future--children and adults."

Eleanor Drago-Severson
Professor of Education Leadership & Adult Learning and Leadership, Teachers College, Columbia University, author of *Helping Teachers Learn, Becoming Adult Learners, Leading Adult Learning, Learning for Leadership* (lead co-author), *Tell me so I can hear you* (lead co-author)

"Ironically, ask any parent or teacher what they want for their children and we all respond the same: we want them to be happy, healthy and to enjoy their lives. Yet, the first stunning impact of this book makes it clear that we have created systems that sabotage those very hopes. In this compelling work, David Gleason articulates the concussing forces that contribute to increasing levels of anxiety, depression and suicidality evident in children and young adults. He then, just as powerfully, offers us the questions that frame opportunities for positive change at personal and systemic levels. With these questions, and with Gleason's clear guidance, a sense of being able to actually impact our students' lives toward greater serenity, health and happiness becomes possible. In this work, David Gleason models for each of us the capacities we all wish for within ourselves, our leaders and our children: the ability to ask tough questions that get to the heart of the matter; the capacity to be brave in naming what is broken, and the insight to create a path toward solutions that are pragmatic *and* enlivening. This is a book I cannot wait to send to my colleagues in the education field, and to the many parents I know who worry constantly about their children."

Maria Sirois, Psy.D. Author of *A Short Course in Happiness After Loss (and Other Dark, Difficult Times)*

AT WHAT COST?

Defending Adolescent Development in Fiercely Competitive Schools

DAVID L. GLEASON, PSY.D.

Foreword by DANIEL J. SIEGEL, M.D.

CONTENTS

Part 1: Great Expectations

Part 2: Pressures, Neurodevelopment, and Costs

Part 3: We All Bear the Cost

FOREWORD

We live in a modern world in which there is now so much rapid change that it is often challenging to find a way to feel confident and comfortable with what the future may hold for us, or for the next generation. If you are a parent of young children, you may feel that deep sense of longing to protect them from harm, to keep them safe and nurture their sense of security. You connect with them, try to provide them the kinds of relationships with you and with their friends, family, and teachers that will support their development as they move toward adolescence and adulthood.

But then something perplexing happens. As our young, devoted children enter their adolescence, they seem to transform from the familiar child to a new individual we sometimes may not easily recognize. In new ways we couldn't have imagined, the science of adolescence is revealing that the brain of an individual going through this important period between childhood dependency and adult responsibility is undergoing major "remodeling" as it prunes down unneeded neural connections formed in childhood and then strengthens remaining circuits through the laying down of myelin. This remodeling enables the specializing of circuits and then their linkage. This linkage of differentiated parts is called "integration" and it allows the adolescent to achieve much more efficient and sophisticated functions.

One way of understanding this integrative period of life is with the acronym, ESSENCE. In adolescence, there is an Emotional Spark of *passion*, a Social Engagement of *collaboration* and *connection*, a Novelty-seeking of *courage*, and a Creative Exploration of *imagination*. This ESSENCE of adolescence is essential for us, as adolescents or adults, to understand in order to navigate this important and necessary time of life.

But if we look at the statistics about modern adolescents in many studies, as David Gleason powerfully does in this wonderful and useful book, we find that instead of schools supporting adolescents' emerging passions, drive for connection and collaboration, courage to do things in new ways, and their creative imaginations, despite our best intentions, we shut them down, make them fear each other's successes, overwork them with the same old kinds of learning, do little to support their creative imaginations, sleep-deprive them, set them up for a sense of inadequacy and competition, and offer them a set of values and goals that research has shown have little to do with much of anything that is positive in life—like well-being, social and emotional intelligence, happiness, or even financial or professional success. With this realization of how things usually are in our high-powered educational programs, do we need to wonder why the levels of anxiety, depression, stress, burnout and even suicide are rising in our teens?

It is understandable that as teachers and parents, we want the best for adolescents in these times of uncertainty. We at least want them to be able to get a job in the future! But we all seem to have focused on the *numbers* that give us a false-sense of certainty: high grade point averages, high standardized test scores, and low acceptance rates at elite colleges. What do these coveted numerical values and goals do for us as adults? They give us an understandably longed for, but unfortunately, temporary and ineffective soothing of our own fears and anxiety. Driven to meet these numbers, we do little to support the integrative growth of our adolescents' brains. Driven to meet these numbers, we do little to provide the kinds of learning that would make our adolescents ready for the uncertainties of the future, and that would develop the skills of resilience. Finally, driven to meet these numbers, we do little to nurture the health and strength of our adolescents' minds. Of course we want to protect our children and offer our teens the best chance of what we hope will be a successful future. But while our intentions are laudable, our efforts and focus are misguided at best, and, if we are honest about the science, actually destructive. No one wants to hear that. But that is what science tells us, and few of us are open to listening—because we long to protect our kids with something we can "guarantee"—like the numbers! Protecting is in our innate instinct as parents, and it is something we can aim for as educators, but it is a clear motivation that is aiming in the wrong direction. In short, when it comes to teaching what really matters in a way that grows brain matter best, we've lost our minds.

Science suggests that a focus of our energy and attention on these matters of numbers is actually doing just the opposite of positive support for many, if not most, of our youth. For example, if we say that only ten to fifteen percent of our students who will get into elite colleges or get certain GPA's or test scores are "successful," then we are condemning the vast majority of our student body, over eighty percent, to feel inadequate—and to experience shame about who they are. We aim for a fixed destination instead of the direction of the journey. We focus on learning facts rather than the joy of learning. In addition, most schools falling prey to this common misplacement of adult anxiety insist on so much homework that our youth, trying to comply with our inhumane quantities of work, are sleep-deprived. And we now know that sleep is a time that our supportive glia cells clean up the inevitable toxins that our neurons produce while they are active during our waking hours. Without enabling enough quality and quantity of sleep, we are literally poisoning our adolescents. Moods plunge, inattention and irritability soar, and memory diminishes. How is that for supporting a healthy sense of self?

At What Cost? Defending Adolescent Development in Fiercely Competitive Schools is a useful science-based review of the situation in which we often find ourselves, whether we are teachers, parents, or students in high-pressure schools. David Gleason's powerful approach uses a research-based technique for gathering data from the adults involved to see why we are all so resistant to change—and then offers ways we can consider opening our own minds to make transformation not just an idea, but a practical reality. This is an essential book for you to read if you work with adolescents in order to support their healthy growth and development. Want to make a difference in the lives of youth, now and for the future? Read this book and take in its important and timely messages. We can all work together to make a huge and sometimes life-saving difference in the way we support adolescents during this important period of their lives. Letting go of our false drive for certainty that has already cost so much for so many is in our hands to do, and this book will give you the foundations to make these crucial changes. How we support our students in nurturing their essence will set them up for a life of lasting resilience and success. We can support the growth of healthy and vibrant minds of adolescents who feel good about themselves, love to learn, and are ready to take on this uncertain world we are handing down to them. Adolescents are our future—and you can help them be the strong, compassionate, and prepared leaders of the world ahead in simple but empowering ways that will be good for them, and good for generations to come!

Daniel J. Siegel, M.D.
Executive Director, Mindsight Institute
New York Times Bestselling Author of *Brainstorm: The Power and Purpose of the Teenage Brain*; and *Mind: A Journey to the Heart of Being Human*

PREFACE

My intent in this book is to raise awareness of the increasingly troubled conditions that adolescents are facing in high-achieving and competitive schools across the United States and all around the world; in particular my focus here is on independent and international schools, but that lens also encompasses public schools that aim to foster competitive excellence among their students, and hence, generate the kinds of pressures I detail.

As a clinical psychologist for over twenty years, I have been working with these pressured and (as a consequence) anxious students, primarily within the context of independent and international schools. While most of the interviews I conducted for this book—and therefore, the examples I include here, too—come from independent and international schools, the pressured and high-stress conditions of which I write apply broadly, again, to many public schools, particularly in the United States. Many affluent-area school districts populated by highly educated and wealthy parents collect high property taxes that contribute to the construction and ongoing support of state-of-the-art public schools, all of which include substantial per-pupil annual expenditures. Further, many of these public schools offer such high-quality resources and exceptional academic instruction that they closely resemble many independent and international schools for which parents pay high tuition for similar resources and academic instruction for their children. In fact, many of these schools have already been termed "epicenters of overachievement"[1] that have subjected too many students to intense pressures, such as "advanced-placement classes galore, [the belief] that their futures hinge on perfect SAT scores and preternatural grade-point averages, [and the reality that] kids here don't get enough sleep."[2] These are the combined pressures that interfere with

---

[1] F. Bruni, "*Best, Brightest—and Saddest,*" *New York Times*, April 11, 2015.
[2] Ibid.

our teenagers' developmental trajectories and threaten their mental and physical health. Thus, though my primary narrative examines independent and international schools, to the degree that any educational aim is one of relentless emphasis on "competitive excellence," this book is directed at that phenomenon of imposing overwhelming pressures on our kids "to succeed," wherever that may be demanded—in independent, international or public schools.

What is of great significance in this book is that throughout my investigations in many independent schools in the United States and in hundreds of international schools around the world, I have found *almost complete unanimity* in how educators and parents associated with these high-achieving schools have responded to my inquiries about "pressures" on students. To an alarming degree, that unanimity is this: while they want—more than anything else—to educate and parent their students in healthy and balanced ways, these caring and dedicated adults admit— albeit unintentionally—to overscheduling, overworking, and, at times, overwhelming their students and teenaged children. Not surprisingly, these same adults—educators and parents alike—also admit to feeling frustrated and disillusioned about these negative practices—frustrated that their own actions have resulted in their overworking and overwhelming these adolescents. It is this conflict—fully intending to educate and parent adolescents in healthy and balanced ways, but at the same time admitting to overscheduling, overworking, and, at times, overwhelming them—that is at the very heart of this book.

As for amelioration of this problem, this book differs in a significant way from studies that have traditionally addressed the problems of over-stressed adolescents. Unlike related studies on the same topic of over-stressed kids, *At What Cost?* is focused *primarily* on helping the educators and parents associated with high-achieving and competitive schools to realize the degree to which *they*—again, unintentionally—play an active role in contributing to the pressure that makes life so stressful for their students. Mainstream approaches to students' academic and social-emotional struggles, by contrast, have historically focused almost exclusively on asking the *students* to change (to put in more study time; to develop better academic and/or "executive function" skills; to pay closer/better attention; to regulate their emotions more effectively, etc.) without also asking the schools—*the adults*—to change. I contend that since it is the *adults* who have admitted to having contributed to this overarching problem, it is *they* who must also engage not only in recognizing their collective impact more fully but, also, in working together to change it.

A number of other influential books, such as Vicki Abeles's *Beyond Measure: Rescuing an Overscheduled, Overtested, Underestimated Generation* (2015), Denise Pope's *Doing School: How We Are Creating a Generation of Stressed Out, Materialistic and Miseducated Students* (2001) and Julie Lythcott-Haims's *How to Raise an Adult: Break Free of the Overparenting Trap and Prepare Your Kid for Success* (2015), accurately and vividly highlight the problem of adolescents in competitive schools who experience too much pressure. Hoping to contribute further to this important conversation, *At What Cost?* emphasizes the very specific, if not precise, roles that the adults—educators and parents—are playing to perpetuate this problem year after year. As one of my adult interviewees stated, "If we actually gave in, and a developmentally reasonable schedule emerged, we might achieve a healthy balance for our students at the cost of our school's distinctiveness; we might lose our edge of excellence and become a vanilla school, and who would want to come to a vanilla school?" Another administrator—a head of school—reinforced this, saying, "Yes, while we are committed to supporting our students' mental and physical health, we are also committed to our reputation as a school, to our brand." These two administrators fully acknowledge—for compelling reasons that are reviewed in detail in *At What Cost?*—being as committed to protecting their schools' reputation, their schools' "brand," as they are to also being committed to educating their students and supporting their mental and physical health. As another administrator remarked to me, "The term 'brand' is the language of marketing, not the language of education." I couldn't agree more. Nonetheless, within the current economically pressured environment, the emphasis on marketing all too often interferes with how adults function in schools, and in turn, risks compromising students' learning and their emotional health and development.

In many of the available books on this topic, such as those books mentioned above, the authors present lists of wise and prudent changes that schools and parents should make for improving these pressured conditions. As many schools have already encountered, however, actually making *and maintaining* these changes is easier said than done. With this in mind, and with the hope of shedding light on this disquieting predicament, in *At What Cost?*, I describe how, too often, schools readily turn to outside experts for solutions to *their own* identified challenges. In so doing, schools deprive *themselves* of the opportunity to *work together* not only to frame the specific nature of their own school's challenges, but also, to generate *their own* solutions. Moreover, by turning to outside authorities, schools deprive *themselves* of the opportunities to grow and develop—*to adapt*—into their own real and lasting changes. While there is certainly room for outside consultants to help guide schools through *their own* adaptive processes, it is the educators and parents themselves who need to work together and generate their own solutions. In fact, it is *that very process* that promotes growth and development for the adults. This "adaptation" then enables the adults to operate and manage their own schools in ways that are unique to them and to their own distinctive school cultures.

Finally, because of my long-standing relationships with many independent and international schools throughout the United States, Europe, and Asia, I know them not only as exceptional schools, but also as institutions with their own autonomy and self-governance processes. Independent and international schools are *not* reliant on town and city property taxes or on local governments for their financial viability or for how they choose to operate their own schools. For this reason, I see this microculture of independent and international schools around the world—of which there are over sixteen thousand (9,160 independent secondary schools in the United States serving an estimated 1.5 million high school students,[3] and 7,017 international schools throughout Europe, Asia, South America, and Africa serving about 1.2 million high school students, all of whom use English as their language for learning[4])—as being some of the best-positioned schools in the world to actually do something about overpressuring adolescents more effectively. Because of their autonomy, these schools do not have to wade through the often frustrating political processes of working with local and state governments. Because of their autonomy, these schools can decide to work together and emerge as true leaders in a much-needed movement to empathize more fully with their adolescent students. They can lead the way.

Indeed, you can lead the way! Whether you are an educator or a parent, and whether you are associated with a US independent school, an international school anywhere in the world, or with a competitive and high-achieving public school, I welcome you to this book. In these pages,

---

[3] http://nces.ed.gov/fastfacts/display.asp?id=372
[4] http://monitor.icef.com/2014/03/new-data-on-international-schools-suggests-continued-strong-growth-2/.

I hope you will find new and challenging insights to consider and discuss; that these insights might inspire your own thinking about making developmentally empathic changes in your school, and, mostly, that you also find hope in the recommendations for how these changes can actually occur. I can assure you that adolescents everywhere will be happier and healthier if these hopes of mine—for you—come true. Thank you for reading *At What Cost?* I welcome your remarks and feedback at www.developmentalempathy.org.

ACKNOWLEDGMENTS

While I wrote every word of this book myself, in a very real way, I did not write it alone. For the past five years, I've had the pleasure of working with one of the finest—most wise and perceptive—book consultants, Barbara Feinberg. Before Barbara and I met, she had been described to me as a "book midwife," implying that working with Barbara would mean that she would help me "give birth" to a book, that she would be able to help me cultivate and organize the many and varied ideas that had been gestating in me for many years, ideas that were still seeking expression. Strikingly, Barbara and I have met in person only a handful of times over the five years that we have been working closely together. The rest of that work has occurred in the context of regular phone calls during which Barbara has encouraged, challenged, and coached me, and has pursued ideas with me quite thoroughly. Throughout these countless conversations, not only have I experienced Barbara's intellect, patience, and warmth, I have also learned a great deal from her. Through all of that, I have, in fact, "given birth" to a book. Thank you, Barbara. I could not have written *this* book without you.

For nearly three of the five years that I have been working on this book, as mentioned earlier in this preface and again in the introduction, I've had the privilege of interviewing numerous educators and parents associated with many, many schools. I can honestly say that not even one of these participants engaged my interviews with anything but their complete openness and integrity: it is their openness that gives this book its authenticity. To all my interviewees, I am grateful for your candidness, for your honesty, and for your many contributions to this book. I hope I have represented your sentiments accurately here. It is important to note that while these interviewees have come from numerous American independent schools, from many European and Asian international schools, as well as from several high-achieving and competitive public high schools, none of the individuals (educators or parents), and none of the schools is identified by name.

I would never have wanted to write this book if I had not had the opportunity to work so closely, for many years, with so many engaging and trusting—but also scared, anxious, and disillusioned—students. I want to thank each and every one of the students with whom I have worked over the years, and particularly, the ones I have described in this book. All of you have taught me so much about what it really means to be a psychologist. Thank you. While each student described in this book is a real student with whom I have interacted in close clinical contact at one time or another, I have taken great pains to disguise them and to maintain their privacy.

Throughout the past six or eight months prior to the release of this book, many friends and colleagues have willingly read my manuscript and have offered critical but very supportive feedback. I'm grateful to Jack Megan, Faith Howland, Ed Zadravec, Harry Parad, Jeff Desjarlais, John Drew, Mike Hanas, Matt DeGreeff, Toby Brewster, Stan Berman, Bill Diskin, Betsey Dempsey, Peter Dempsey, Maryellen Kennedy, Bob Brooks, David Rost, Stephen Murdock, Bob Kegan, Lisa Lahey, Michael Thompson, Yong Zhao, Ellie Drago-Severson, Dan Siegel, Rick Hardy, and to two of my family members—my son, Danny Gleason, and my wife, Amy Gleason. Thank you all for your honest and caring feedback. Your comments and reactions have been invaluable to me, and they have contributed significantly to how this book has evolved.

Finally, I am proud and grateful to say that every member of my immediate family has participated in this book in one way or another. My younger son, Stephen Gleason, designed and created the cover art for the book you are now holding in your hands. Thank you, Stevie! My daughter, Sara Gleason, nominated me to be a speaker at the annual Connecticut College TEDx Conference, which led to my giving a TEDx Talk in April of 2016. That talk—available on YouTube—is a brief summary of this book and serves as great way to promote this important topic. Thank you, Sara! My older son, Daniel Gleason, designed and created my new website, www.developmentalempathy.org, which now serves as an online home for my blog, related media, schedule, and for this book. Thank you, Danny! Finally, my wife, Amy Gleason, has not only read and reread every page of every draft, but she has also remained her steady and dependable self, thereby providing unwavering support throughout this whole endeavor. As a first-time author, I experienced many challenges in the process of developing and writing this book. Just as in every other endeavor we have faced together in our twenty-eight years of marriage, Amy has selflessly encouraged my efforts and has helped me find the right "voice" in my writing. Without a doubt, this book reflects Amy's carefully considered input, and it is much better for it. Thank you, Amy!

In the sacred words of the twenty-third Psalm, "My cup runneth over." I am blessed to be part of such a loving and supportive family. I love each of you more than mere words can express, and I dedicate this book to you.

David Gleason
December, 2016

PART 1

Great Expectations

In a recent session, Michaela, a seventh-grader at an academically rigorous middle school, took her usual seat on the couch in my office. She grabbed the Rubik's Twist toy and quickly twisted it into a snake-shaped figure, and as she began talking, twisted it again into a perfect square and held it up to frame her face. "I saw a bunch of my third grade friends in town the other day … and it made me feel kinda sad."

"Why?" I asked.

"It was great to see them but …"

"But what?"

"But … well … I felt kinda left out … cuz they're like hangin'out together all the time … they get out of school at two thirty every day … and I don't get out until like five or five thirty … and then I have all this homework … and all this stress." We talked more about Michaela's academic struggles, about her earning Cs on every math test despite her studying "so hard" for every one, and about Michaela's feeling "so frustrated about that!" Because she feels so overscheduled—school, sports, tutoring, homework—Michaela often feels alone and isolated, or, as she reports, "left out," feelings that were unexpectedly amplified when she saw friends from four years ago, "friends" that Michaela now imagines are enjoying life much more than she is.

"Michaela, can I ask you something," I queried.

"Sure," she replied.

Reaching to my bookcase, I grasped a replica of Professor Dumbledore's wand that I had purchased recently at the Harry Potter Theme Park. Handing the wand to Michaela, I said, "This wand gives you the power to walk out of your competitive school today, and to join your friends from third grade in their fun-filled lives right now. If you go, you, too, could get out at two thirty every day, have much less homework, and resume the childhood you seem to be missing. Think about it. Would you go?"

Michaela stared at me, stunned, and eventually uttered, "I don't know. It would be sad to just leave my friends … and … I would miss the seventh-grade trip to New York … and the big eighth-grade year next year, the opportunity to be like seniors at the school. And I'll be applying to [secondary] schools next year … so how would it look if I just quit this school in the middle of seventh grade?"

Michaela felt stuck. On the one hand, she longed for the freedom that she imagined her old friends were now experiencing. On the other hand, she also wanted the privileges of the New York class trip, the eighth-grade "senior status," and perhaps, most of all, the luxury of applying to competitive independent secondary schools as a student in good standing from this similarly rigorous middle school. Michaela had already experienced "buy in" to this hyperschooling culture, one that has been characterized by subjecting children and adolescents to "excessive schooling" at younger and younger ages so they will be able "to compete in the global market place."[5] This trend of hyperschooling has "negative implications for the social and emotional development of children and adolescents,"[6] as the American Academy of Pediatrics warns of the relationship between increased depression and anxiety in children and the lack of the simple childhood pleasure of play.[7] For the record, Michaela is twelve years old, and she is *not* thinking about her status in the global marketplace. Nonetheless, Michaela's hyperschooling—also referred to as "the full-time job of schooling"[8]—seems not only developmentally inappropriate, but also completely out of sync with what Michaela wants and with what is best for her now, as a twelve-year-old child. Sadly, though, because of her established acquiescence to this hyperschooling culture, even though Michaela frequently feels sad and stressed, she is not so ready to give it up.

I tested her a bit more. "Michaela, let's just say that you *did* walk out of your school tomorrow. What would you do with all that time that you wouldn't be in school or doing homework?"

"Well … I'd dance more … I used to take dance lessons until third grade but I had to stop because I didn't have enough time when I got to this school. And I'd just hang out more … I'd have more playdates with

---

[5] www.nebraskafamilyforum.org, August 10, 2011
[6] Ibid.
[7] Ibid.
[8] Ibid.

my friends ... maybe I'd play on another sports team ... like town soccer or something."

As Michaela spoke freely of how she might spend her time if she were not attending her rigorous middle school, I thought, *That's how she should be spending more of her childhood!* A part of Michaela knew that, too, while another part of her had already "bought in" to this competitive-school culture. Michaela was also trying to comply with her parents' hopes and dreams for her, that she will be able to maintain the comfortable life later they have tried to give her now.

"Michaela, at what cost do you attend this competitive school? What are the personal costs for you?"

Without a second thought, Michaela said, "Free time and relaxation."

"Is it worth it? Is this school worth that price?" I asked.

"I don't know," Michaela replied. "I really don't know."

Michaela's ambivalence was poignant. As a twelve-year-old girl, Michaela understood that at this stage in her life, she *should* be dancing more, that she *should* be having more playdates and *should* be hanging out more with her friends. However, because she was already engrossed in this competitive educational track, Michaela had also come to understand—and to want—the many benefits she had already earned, and she didn't want to give those up.

The combined external influences of school, parents, and peers already had a grip on Michaela's early-adolescent mind-set, rendering her vulnerable to ... and tolerant of ... "all this stress" that she accepted as one of the effects of this hyperschooling environment,[9] an effect to which she had already grown rather accustomed.

Clinical Observations and Increasing Rates of Adolescent Depression

Listening to, and counseling with, adolescents is as much about hearing what they say and don't say as it is about observing what they do and don't do. In this way, my work has always involved listening closely to adolescents' words as well as observing and translating their behavior, striving to understand their feelings, and, ultimately, trying to empathize with them and offer effective interventions and support. This book reflects my

---

[9] Ibid.

effort to empathize with adolescents on a larger scale, and to invite you, my readers, to do the same.

I work closely with adolescents who feel stressed and pressured, conditions that manifest as academic, emotional, and/or behavioral problems that interfere with what they are trying to accomplish or with whom they're trying to be. From that perspective, I have written this book to be an account, if not a defense, of adolescents who experience too much pressure, and what *we*—the adults who educate and parent them—can begin to do about it.

The adolescents described here are in schools where "feeling stressed and pressured" has become routine. As the applications to selective colleges have steadily increased while the admission rates at those same colleges have steadily decreased, the students *competing* for those few selective places feel more and more stressed and pressured—the effects of hyperschooling. Sadly, as we saw with Michaela, these effects are not just tolerated, they have become "the new normal." Further, as you will soon see for yourself, if these high-achieving and competitive schools—in close collaboration with parents—do *not* support this hyperschooling culture in some way—albeit unintentionally—they risk being perceived as intellectually soft and lacking in rigor, perceptions that could damage their reputations, lead to lower ratings, and result in lower enrollments. While these are, indeed, unsettling concerns for educators and parents to consider, it is the *students* who bear the burden of these hyperschooling practices, and it is they whom I have been treating since the start of my career.

After more than twenty years of this challenging but rewarding work, I have grown increasingly alarmed at what I'm *still* hearing and observing. More and more students say, with unsettled words and disturbing behavior, that they're feeling too pressured and frequently overwhelmed, and that they're also trying their best. Too often, however, "their best" just isn't enough. Not surprisingly, my clinical observations are consistent with current trends in the United States and throughout the world. According to Mental Health America, "Adolescent depression is increasing at an alarming rate. Recent surveys indicate that as many as one in five teens suffers from clinical depression."[10] Further, according to a May 2014 report from the World Health Organization, "Globally, depression is the number one cause of illness and disability" for adolescents, and "half of

---

[10] www.mentalhealthamerica.net/conditions/depression-teens.

all people who develop mental disorders have their first symptoms by the age of fourteen."[11]

Most of my young clients admit to having tried to talk with adults in their lives—to their parents, teachers, coaches, advisors, and guidance counselors—about how pressured they feel, but from these students' perspectives, nothing seems to change. In all honesty, many students report that their pressures only seem to intensify, as more and more demands get piled on to their already-frenetic schedules. Feeling overwhelmed, unheard, and at times disillusioned, many students act out their feelings of frustration, anger, fear, and shame in a variety of behavioral ways. Some develop persistent symptoms of anxiety and depression. Others "shut down," refuse to do their schoolwork, and some exhibit previously nonexistent symptoms of attentional disorders— failing to play close attention to details, making careless mistakes, difficulty sustaining attention, appearing not to be listening, not following through on instructions or finishing homework[12]—many students turn to alcohol and marijuana for intermittent relief, while others lash out, using physical aggression or social exclusion to offset their own underlying vulnerability. Some students starve themselves or develop chronic bulimic behaviors while others repeatedly cut or burn themselves. Tragically, some commit suicide.

As a younger and less experienced psychologist, when I first listened and tried to intervene with these students, I saw their troubles as manifestations of their particular vulnerabilities, as indicators of these unlucky students' inabilities to meet the demands of these hyperschooling environments. At this point, however, for reasons that will become clearer throughout this book, I now see these students' troubles as manifestations of their anxious, and sometimes desperate, attempts—individually and collectively—to get *our* attention to help them cope with the intensifying pressures that, to them, seem ubiquitous, pressures that put *all* students who attend these schools— not just the "unlucky few" who have presented in my office—in jeopardy.

Worldwide Phenomenon

A few years ago, I presented a workshop at an international schools conference in Bangkok, Thailand—one of many I would be giving in various

---

[11] www.who.int/mediacentre/news/releases/2014/focus-adolescent-health/en/.

[12] *Diagnostic and Statistical Manual of Mental Disorders*, 5th ed. (Washington, DC, & London, England. American Psychiatric Association, 2013), 59.

parts of the world—about developing effective interventions for counseling vulnerable adolescents. At that time, I was eager to learn about the struggling students in those international schools, and to see if their struggles were similar to those of the students I had known in American schools. As part of that workshop, I asked my conference attendees to identify the symptoms of the students who were struggling most in their schools. Their list read as follows: "lack of motivation, sleep deprivation, procrastination, anxiety and depression, self-harming behaviors, overwhelmed by simultaneous bombardment of demands, academic underachievement, substance abuse, eating disorders, feeling overscheduled and expected to manage without negative effects, expectations too high, excessive computer gaming, and suicide."

When I first encountered their list, I have to admit, I felt stunned. I was far from home, in Thailand, meeting with educators from about eighty different international schools from that region of Asia. I was amazed that their observations about their students could have been about the many troubled students I had seen over the years of working with American adolescents. While I had certainly anticipated some overlap between their observations and mine, I had not expected an *identical* list of symptoms. Subsequently, I continued to present the same workshop at numerous schools and other conferences in other areas of Asia and Europe. In these additional workshops, I have encountered, again and again, the same list of symptoms. Clearly, the students in international schools reveal their troubles with the same disturbing symptoms as the students in American schools do.

For many readers, this conclusion may not seem that surprising. After all, since there are developmental and cultural similarities among teenagers who attend high-achieving secondary schools all around the world, the idea that teenagers in America and teenagers in Europe and Asia would experience anxiety and depression similarly, or that they would act out in similarly disturbing ways does, in fact, seem quite logical. For me, however, it was the unexpected realization of the scale of the problem, the universality of it, that I found so unsettling. For me, it was the plain and simple insight that *so many* teenagers in *so many* rigorous secondary schools everywhere were (still are) manifesting with *so many* of the same disturbing problems.

For health-care providers, among the many ways to consider the seriousness of any presenting problem, and from there to determine an appropriate treatment plan, is to consider three basic diagnostic criteria: the *frequency* with which a problem occurs, the *intensity* of its occurrence, and/ or its *duration*—for how long has this problem been occurring? As I began to comprehend the scale of these school-related adolescent problems, I realized that they would get high scores for all three diagnostic criteria: they occur frequently to many students in competitive schools all around the world; they occur intensely—sometimes dangerously—for some of these students, and they have been occurring for many years.

With this overall realization, I began to wonder, "Why are so many kids, in so many schools all around the world, struggling in such serious ways?" While most schools have on-staff counselors and learning specialists who are available to "treat" these students' emotional and/or academic problems, many of the students' problems are simply too severe, and sometimes too chronic, for these school professionals to manage on their own. Furthermore, given the global scale of these student problems, I began to wonder, have *we* considered looking closely at what *we* are doing that might be contributing to our students' difficulties? Rather than remaining only reactive to our students' problems by providing counseling and learning support *after* the problems have surfaced, is it possible for us to be more proactive by developing creative approaches for preventing these problems from happening? Specifically, I couldn't help but ask: Are there changes *we* should be making that would help our students to feel less pressured?

It was this particular question that led me to consider using the *Immunity to Change* paradigm[13] to explore this central question in greater depth. Having studied for several years with the authors of *Immunity to Change*, Drs. Robert Kegan and Lisa Lahey, I already knew that paradigm to be a unique and powerful tool used widely with individuals and organizations throughout the fields of business, health care, and education, a tool that enables participants to identify the puzzling gap between their earnest intentions to change and the various obstacles they face—conscious and unconscious—that typically make real and lasting change so difficult.[14] The *Immunity to Change* protocol by which I have explored my central question—its complete step-by-step interview—can be viewed in chapter 2. I feel an enormous debt of gratitude to Drs. Kegan and Lahey, as it is their many years of research in the fields of human growth and development and

---

[13] R. Kegan and L. Lahey, *Immunity to Change: How to Overcome It and Unlock the Potential in Yourself and Your Organization* (Boston, MA. Harvard Business Review Press, January 2009).

[14] Ibid., 2.

in individual and organizational change that has enabled me to explore my questions so thoroughly.

Macroeconomic and Cultural Pressures

I am well aware that the fierce competition that now faces adolescents attending rigorous and competitive schools is much bigger than the schools themselves, and that all high-achieving and highly ranked schools are subject to powerful, if not prevailing, economic and cultural influences that appear to be driving the competition in the first place. For example, several recent *New York Times* articles have highlighted the clusters of suicides that have occurred in numerous "ultrahigh-achieving communities"[15] throughout the United States where "the culture of best in class is playing out"[16] in harmful and dangerous ways. In these communities, says Dr. Denise Pope, Senior Lecturer at Stanford University, students are "hearing the overriding message that only the best will do—in grades, test scores, sports, art, college ... in everything."[17] Further, this message seems intensified by the fact that in many of these schools, there is "a concentrated number of very, very talented kids"[18] who make it harder and harder for any of them to stand out. Consequently, many students not only absorb but wholly internalize overly competitive mind-sets, distilled from their parents and teachers and from the culture at large, that manifest as internal exigencies, or as expectations they *must* achieve. Essentially, the more students hear the message that "only the best will do," the more they acquiesce to that mind-set and try to function accordingly. For many students, this mind-set becomes a setup. As noted by Diane Kapp in a recent *UpShot* radio interview in San Francisco, more and more students are "chasing a goal that has been imposed on them by society, or by their parents, and they've completely internalized it so they now expect it of themselves."[19] As *New York Times* writer Matt Richtel describes, "It puts enormous pressure on a school, or a community, [but mostly on students] when such consistent,

---

[15] M. Richtel, "Push, Don't Crush, the Students," www.nytimes.com, April 24, 2015.
[16] Ibid.
[17] Ibid.
[18] D. Kapp,, *Upshot* interview, *"Why Are Palo Alto Kids Killing Themselves?"* San Francisco *Magazine*, May 14, 2015.
[19] Ibid.

across-the-board greatness becomes a baseline of sorts, [or of what one parent] described as a culture of 'not just excellence but uber-excellence.'"[20]

Why is this happening? Why the need for such "ultrahigh-achievement and uber-excellence?" Richtel cites Dr. Morton Silverman, a psychiatrist and senior science advisor to the Suicide Prevention Resource Center, as claiming that these pressures may reflect "a sense of terror about the future among both students and parents."[21] Further, as Richtel notes, "with the economy in flux and the income gap growing, parents don't see a clear path anymore to financial stability"[22] for their children.

Reinforcing this point in her book *Monoculture: How One Story Is Changing Everything*, F. S. Michaels provides a compelling summary of the economic conditions to which Richtel has alluded. As Michaels notes, "back in the 1950s the relationship between employees and their companies involved commitment and reciprocity; workers were committed to the job in return for wages and promotions, and the company was committed to its workers in return for their hard work and loyalty. That long-term employment relationship, with its stability, regular promotions, and raises, let employees plan on owning a home and sending their children to college or university. In exchange, workers were loyal and didn't move around much, staying with the same company in the same city, maybe for decades."[23] While this kind of stability and financial predictability may reflect the economy in which many of our parents raised us—their baby boomer children—it certainly does not reflect the economy of today.

As Michaels describes further, because "corporations [now] compete in a global market ... they are under pressure to compete efficiently and stay attractive to [global] investors ... and one way [of competing efficiently] is to have more flexible workforces, and to be less tied to [their] employees. Since labor costs represent a major expense to most companies, hiring employees when there's work and laying them off when the work slows down can help firms stay competitive. That means the employment relationship that once stretched out into the future isn't on the table anymore."[24] Consequently, "corporations and employees are no longer that committed

---

[20] M. Richtel, "Push, Don't Crush, the Students."

[21] Ibid.

[22] Ibid.

[23] F. S. Michaels, *Monoculture: How One Story Is Changing Everything* (Kamloops, British Columbia, Red Clover Press, 2011). 23.

[24] Ibid.

to each other."[25] According to Michaels, it is this story—"the economic story"—that is changing everything, and from what my interviews have shown, even extraordinary secondary schools are vulnerable to these prevailing economic conditions.

Understandably, given the established correlation between higher education levels and higher income levels, there is a hope—perhaps an illusion—that if a student attends one of the best secondary schools, then he or she will get admitted to one of the best colleges or universities, will then get one of the best jobs, make the most money, and, thereby, be happy and safe, and avoid future economic trouble. This illusory thinking may provide temporary comfort from the "sense of terror about the future" described earlier by Dr. Silverman, but it does not—it cannot—provide guarantees. Not only is real life not that predictable, but also, examples abound of elite-college graduates who struggle to find work, and of highly successful individuals who attended less well-known colleges or who never even earned a college degree. There are no guarantees, but we hedge our bets, nonetheless, in an effort to manage our anxieties about our children's future.

In his most recent book, *Creative Schools: The Grassroots Revolution That's Transforming Education*, Dr. Ken Robinson describes how these conditions are fueling our anxieties in today's economic environment. As Robinson states, "The standards movement [characterized by raising academic standards, preparing students for future employment, addressing overseas competition, and high-stakes testing] is not meeting the economic challenges we face."[26] Further, despite increased academic standards and high-stakes testing, "youth unemployment around the world is at record levels. There are about six hundred million people on Earth between the ages of fifteen and twenty-four. About seventy-three million of them are long-term unemployed. That's the largest number ever recorded—nearly 13 percent of the population in that age group."[27] Alarmingly—and particularly germane to many students attending high-achieving secondary schools—Robinson reports that this "blight of unemployment is even affecting young people who've done everything that was expected of them and graduated from college. Between 1950 and 1980, a college degree was

---

[25] Ibid.
[26] K. Robinson and L. Aronica, *Creative Schools: The Grassroots Revolution That's Transforming Education* (New York, Viking, 2015), 14.
[27] Ibid.

pretty much a guarantee of a good job. If you had a degree, employers formed a line to interview you. They don't now. The essential problem is not the quality of degrees, but the quantity."[28] Robinson asserts, "In a world bristling with graduates, a college degree is no longer the distinction it once was."[29]

How do these conditions affect students who attend high-achieving secondary schools? Since many of these students are already aware that "a college degree is no longer the distinction it once was," the combination of their inborn drive for "distinction" and their distilled mind-set that "only the best will do" leads them—and many educators and parents, too—to the perception that *only* a degree from one of the most selective colleges will provide them with the "distinction" they crave and the benchmark they think they need to live a successful life in the future.

Our Own Double-Bind

Equipped with the *Immunity to Change* paradigm, I have traveled extensively throughout the United States, Europe, and Asia, and have interviewed hundreds of educators and parents associated with many, many schools. As you will soon see for yourself, within the structure of the *Immunity to Change* paradigm, these dedicated and honest educators and parents, almost uniformly, have openly admitted to regularly putting too much pressure on their students and children. Further, these same adults have also acknowledged feeling deeply troubled by these admissions, as they recognize that putting too much pressure on these adolescents conflicts directly with their original intentions of educating and parenting in healthy and balanced ways. Finally, compelled by their fears associated with the aforementioned economic and cultural influences, these same adults openly acknowledged their underlying assumption that if they *didn't* impose all that pressure, then their students and children wouldn't get in to the most selective colleges, and that they—the adults—would then feel like failures as either educators or parents.

This unpopular but real predicament reflects a true double bind for us. As a population of well-intended professional educators and committed parents all around the world, we are acting in ways that compromise our

---

[28] Ibid., 15.
[29] Ibid.

very intentions. On the one hand, we feel deeply committed to educating and parenting our students/children in healthy and balanced ways. On the other hand, under the weight of so much economic and cultural pressure, we simultaneously find ourselves overscheduling, overworking, and at times, overwhelming our students and children with *un*healthy and *un*-balanced practices.

Something is very wrong here. Regardless of how we understand, explain, or even justify our adult functioning in response to economic and cultural pressures, it still results frequently in too much pressure for our students, pressure that often translates to increasing competition among and between them. Don't misinterpret me here: pressure to succeed, in and of itself, is not necessarily unhealthy. However, too much pressure—for anyone, but especially for still-developing children and adolescents—can be dangerous.

Most students in demanding secondary schools experience too much pressure at one time or another, and, therefore, may pay a short-term cognitive, emotional, or even physical price. For example, it is well documented that excessive stress activates the human nervous system and puts its entire metabolism on high alert, leading to temporary compromises in attention, memory, and learning, as well as to increased risk of anxiety and depression.[30] This automatic reaction reflects the body's adaptive response to short-term stress, but if the stress is ongoing, it can be highly problematic.[31]

As mentioned above, it is important to acknowledge that stress, or "pressure," per se, is not always destructive. In fact, we have known for over one hundred years that *some* pressure is actually necessary to achieve optimal performance.[32] In small doses, pressure can help individuals of all ages to perform more effectively and motivate them to do their best.[33] However, when pressure is chronic—as it is for many students in competitive school environments—it can develop insidiously into a state of "too much pressure," and can be harmful to adolescents' still-developing minds

---

[30] C. Bergland, "Cortisol: Why "The Stress Hormone" Is Public Enemy No. 1," *The Athlete's Way*. Jan. 22, 2013.

[31] D. J. Seigel, *Mindsight: The New Science Of Personal Transformation* (New York, Bantam Books, 2011), 18.

[32] R. M. Yerkes and J. D. Dodson, "The relation of strength of stimulus to rapidity of habit-formation," *Journal of Comparative Neurology and Psychology* 18 (1908): 459–82.

[33] *Stress Symptoms, Signs, and Causes: The Effects of Stress Overload and What You Can Do About It*, Helpguide.org.

and bodies. Specifically, facing constantly pressured conditions in which effective coping is hindered can "be toxic to the growing brain and interfere with proper growth."[34]

From my inquiries in schools around the world, I have observed that many adolescents in these hyperschooling environments confront very similar pressures. Given adolescents' normal developmental variation with respect to both their *ability* to deal with these pressures, as well as to their *readiness* to deal with them, many of these students simply collapse under the weight of too much pressure that occurs too early in their lives. Further, these intensely demanding and chronic pressures often outweigh schools' ancillary support services, thereby rendering *all* students vulnerable, at one time or another, to emotional and behavioral trouble. None of these students signed up for this.

Unprecedented Knowledge of Adolescent Brain Development

Many readers may acknowledge that these so-called "unhealthy and unbal-anced" practices have been going on in competitive schools for many years, and may then ask, "Why make such a fuss about them now?"

Until very recently, most of our educational and parenting practices have been based primarily on theories about human growth and develop-ment. Now, however, thanks to advances in neuroimaging over the past ten to fifteen years, we can see—noninvasively—inside the living brains of young adolescents. While the theories that have guided us for decades have certainly been helpful, every one of them lacked the precision—the neuro-biological facts—that neuroimaging can now provide. With ever-increasing exactness, we know more than ever before about adolescents' brain devel-opment. With these new and extraordinary insights, we now know too much *not* to be acting in ways that are more developmentally empathic and "in sync" with human brain development.

As mentioned earlier, most schools have implemented reactive ways of supporting their troubled students. Specifically, they have provided ac-cess to professional counselors as well as additional instruction by learn-ing support specialists. While these services will always be necessary to some degree, in light of what we now know about adolescent brain

---

[34] Seigel, *Mindsight*, 18.

development—particularly as the "fierce competition" increases and the pressure on students intensifies—we need to work together to develop proactive ways of supporting students in a collective effort to prevent these pressures from harming them. Since the problem of "too much pressure" on our students does not seem to be going away, it is up to us, the adults who educate and parent them, to both acknowledge this problem and work together to try to change it.

Call to Action

You may be asking, "What would proactive support look like in our school?" "What kind of changes are you asking us to make?" "How do you expect *us* to change when the economic and cultural pressures that got us here still hold sway?"

In the final chapters of this book, I will address these questions in greater detail. For now, though, let's just acknowledge that "the pressures that got us here" are not going away anytime soon, but our students need us to try to change now. We cannot wait for these pressured conditions to "go away": we need to try to begin operating in ways that not only prepare adolescents for productive and meaningful futures, but also, that defend and protect them, as they are not in any position to do that for themselves. We are the adults: our students look to *us* not only to educate them but, also, to take care of them.

Because of each school's uniqueness, I know that I do *not* know the precise changes that would be appropriate for every school. While I believe that all competitive secondary schools need to deliberate on these concerns, the specifics of how each school prioritizes which changes to make, and in what order to make them, can only be determined from within each school's particular culture and history. As many will agree, many of these schools share remarkable similarities. Nonetheless, each one still operates according to its own distinctive qualities and traditions, and these distinguishing features must be taken into account as each school considers its own specific changes.

Having said that, I acknowledge that I have explored these topics in schools around the world, and have also heard numerous suggestions from school administrators, teachers, and parents along the way. Although I cannot prescribe specific changes, I will provide a list of what I consider "supportive strategies" and recommendations that reflect countless educators' and parents' empathic insights into adolescent development. Each strategy reflects a specific area of adolescent functioning that is "in flux" and, therefore, developmentally vulnerable during the early adolescent years, and for that reason, should be factored in to any school's overall approach to making developmentally appropriate changes. With these intervention guidelines, I hope that individual schools will prioritize which aspects of adolescent functioning—within their school—need the most developmentally oriented adjustment. The end of the book provides a specific process by which schools can work either individually or collectively toward making these adaptive changes.

It is worth acknowledging that it would be risky for one school—or even for just a few schools—to make these changes in isolation. However, as we all know, there is certainly strength in numbers. While independent, international, and high-achieving public schools may reflect a minority of schools relative to all secondary schools throughout the world, as stated above, these schools are well-recognized for having "a concentrated number of very, very talented kids"[35] such that the most selective colleges and universities rely on students from *these* schools to apply to them. From this perspective, we are a small but very strong group of educators who, collectively, have leverage and can afford to take a stand on educating our students in developmentally empathic ways. Plus, what college or university would not want to admit healthier and less stressed-out kids?

In summary, with this book, I invite educators and parents everywhere into a dialogue about this regrettable bind we are in, and that we ask ourselves, "At what cost to our students, to our schools, and to ourselves, do we continue to operate within the assumption that this bind is bigger than we are, and that we are powerless and not able to address it?" My sole intention is to bring this bind to our collective attention with the hope that we will not only acknowledge it but, also, work together to change it. To be sure, just acknowledging this bind is unsettling. However, when we consider how this bind may be compromising the health and development of our students and children, it takes on a whole new meaning and challenges *us* to change. Without a doubt, the last thing any of us wants is to knowingly contribute to our students' and children's troubles.

Although the macroeconomic and cultural pressures are so much

---

[35] Kapp, *Upshot* interview.

bigger than the microculture of rigorous and competitive secondary schools, as I mentioned in the preface, my focus on these schools now is due to the fact that these are the schools in which most of my professional experience has been. That said, without a doubt, the conditions described in this book reflect a categorical hyperschooling tendency that applies broadly—to high-achieving independent, international, and public schools in the United States and around the world—to *any* school in which students face (from their perspective) insurmountable pressures that interfere with their emotional and physical health and development.

After more than twenty years of working in many of these extraordinary schools, I have come to know them as having significant human, intellectual, and financial resources such that they—we—may be some of the best positioned schools in the world to actually do something about this bind, to work together and emerge as true leaders in a much-needed movement to empathize more fully with our adolescent students. I am reminded of Margaret Mead's famous quotation: "Never doubt that a small group of thoughtful, committed citizens can change the world; indeed, it's the only thing that ever has."

I feel confident that our microculture of rigorous and competitive secondary schools is that "small group of thoughtful, committed citizens" who "can change [the educational] world," by changing how we operate to reflect our collective commitment to respecting our students' developmental capacities, to respecting who they are.

CHAPTER 1
Passport to a Better Life?

Each year, thousands of young and aspiring teenagers apply for admission to independent and international secondary schools throughout the world. The numbers are compelling. For example, at some of the larger and most prestigious New England schools, it is common to receive over twenty-five hundred applications for about 350 positions in the ninth and tenth grades. Several smaller schools receive upwards of fifteen hundred applications for roughly 150 combined positions for ninth and tenth grades. Overall, most of these schools accept about 15 to 20 percent of their applicants in order to matriculate their incoming ninth- and tenth-graders. These schools are in very high demand.

The appeal for these high-performance schools far exceeds the New England area. A recent *New York Times* article reported that "International Schools Boom as More Seek Education in English."[36] In that piece, Joyce Lau noted that "a century ago, international schools were small, elite replicas of Western schools for the generally white, rich children of parents posted in 'exotic' locales."[37] However, "as developed nations have become wealthier and as the world has become more multicultural, international schools have boomed. According to ISC Research in Britain, there are now sixty-four hundred international schools all over the globe. In a decade, that number is expected to almost double."[38]

In an earlier article, "International Schools in China Point Students to the West," Lucy Hornby-Reuters reported that "upwardly mobile Chinese

---

[36] J. Lau, "International Schools Boom as More Seek Education in English," *New York Times*, April 29, 2013.

[37] Ibid.

[38] Ibid.

parents are willing to pay as much as 260,000 renminbi, or about $42,000, a year for a Western-style education and a possible ticket to a college overseas for their children."[39] Further, Hornby-Reuters noted that "the number of international schools registered in mainland China has soared in the past 12 years, to 338, from 22," and that "enrollment has risen 25 times in the same period, to 184,073 students." Essentially, "parents who can afford the international schools say it is a passport to a better life for their children, despite much higher costs."[40]

The search for rigorous and high-achieving schools is not new. Nearly thirty years ago, in their book *Preparing for Power: America's Elite Boarding Schools*, Cookson and Hodges-Persell[41] described American boarding schools that were modeled deliberately after English "public schools" such as Eton College and Harrow School. Cookson and Hodges-Persell wrote, "As total institutions in aesthetic surroundings, many [elite independent] schools seem almost like island paradises within the larger educational system."[42]

Understandably, these institutions are alluring for many reasons. Further, I fully acknowledge that for many students, these schools do, indeed, serve as "passports to a better life." For numerous others, however, that is not the case. In this section, we examine the most desirable features of these extraordinary schools, and then consider how for some students, these features come with a heavy cost.

Academic Excellence

In many independent and international schools, the average class size is ten to fifteen students. Further, classes are often taught around large oval tables or in small classrooms where students and their teacher engage in stimulating discussions about the course material. In these intimate learning environments, all students get highly individualized attention because of the low student-to-teacher ratio, a ratio that is much lower than that

---

[39] L. Hornby-Reuters, "International Schools in China Point Students to the West," *New York Times*, January 14, 2013.
[40] Ibid.
[41] P. W. Cookson and C. Hodges-Persell, *Preparing for Power: America's Elite Boarding Schools* (New York, Basic Books, 1987).
[42] Ibid., 48.

of most US public schools (20:1) and of many schools in Asia and South America (30:1).[43]

Adding to this alluring profile is the presence of a dedicated and highly skilled faculty. Many faculty members have advanced degrees and many years of teaching experience. Further, they not only teach their classes, but also, they coach sports, direct various musical or theatrical performances, lead dormitories, and meet with their advisees on a weekly basis ... all in addition to trying to maintain their own personal lives with their families, many of whom live on campus. These faculty members are a dedicated group, committed with vocation-like energy to working and, oftentimes, living among their teenaged students.

Typically, these schools offer ample courses in English, math, science, foreign language, social sciences, and art, as well as a variety of advanced placement (AP) and/or international baccalaureate (IB) courses. In addition, all students work closely with an advisor, a faculty member who not only guides the student's course selections, but also who works to develop a close personal connection. Courtney, a recent graduate, reflected on her relationship with her advisor, Mrs. Thompson. "We met every week and would spend time just chatting and checking in. I always looked forward to our meetings and felt comfortable talking to her about anything! It was so helpful to have such a supportive and caring adult presence through all the ups and downs of my school life. Even a couple years after graduation, I am still very close with Mrs. Thompson." Without a doubt, the opportunity to learn within such an enriched academic curriculum, combined with the prospect of developing a close personal connection with an advisor, adds to the appeal of these environments.

Finally, perhaps one of the most attractive qualities about these schools is the endemic mindset among the students that "it's cool to be smart." Sadly, in many schools, numerous once-motivated students deliberately surrender their intellectual abilities and academic interests in order to gain or maintain peer acceptance. For most adolescents, having friends is a paramount concern, and some have been willing to "dumb down" in the interest of securing or maintaining peer connections. In high-achieving schools, however, already described as those that have a "concentrated number of very, very talented kids,"[44] being surrounded by like-minded

---

[43] http://www.oecd.org/edu/skills-beyond-school/48631144.pdf.
[44] Kapp, *UpShot* interview.

peers is a blessing, a positive and fully incorporated influence for academic success.

Access to Resources

Independent and international school websites offer picturesque examples of the "aesthetic surroundings" that "seem almost like island paradises," as described Cookson and Persell above. Large grassy areas; impressive dormitories, and administration and classroom buildings; and majestic chapels typically characterize these schools. Students and teachers often gather in an array of spacious public areas during their time between classes, socializing with one another and contributing to the diverse community of adults and students who come from many US states and foreign countries. It is within this "aesthetic surround" that these schools conduct their stated mission of helping each student develop to her or his full potential.

The combined wealth and commitment to academic excellence of these schools are evident in the facilities they provide. For example, in addition to their state-of-the art classrooms—equipped with smartboards and other advanced audiovisual technology—many schools feature observatories, greenhouses, and robotics labs, as well as numerous spacious study and work spaces.

While most of these schools are now nondenominational schools, many still feature a majestic chapel where the entire school gathers as a community several times each week. In this space, over the course of the full school year, seniors—and sometimes, faculty members—address the entire school with deeply personal messages. This cherished tradition enables seniors to simultaneously rise to the occasion of addressing the entire school and to officially leave their mark on their school as a whole.[45]

After school, most students proceed to a wide range of athletic and artistic activities. Interscholastic teams that accommodate various skill levels appeal to students of varying athletic abilities. Sports teams typically practice on well-manicured fields, row crew on nearby rivers and scenic ponds, exercise in fully equipped fitness centers, and many play matches on turf fields. Some of these schools have indoor swimming pools; many have several international squash courts, indoor hockey rinks, and well-maintained basketball courts, as well as tennis courts and large dance studios.

---

[45] http://www.concordacademy.org/admissions/campus.aspx.

In addition to these exceptional athletic facilities, arts programs designed to "inspire students to explore their creativity and encourage self-expression"[46] are standard in these schools, as they endorse the "belief that artistic sensibility is a vital part of a well-rounded education."[47] Visual arts students enroll in various design, drawing and painting, and graphic arts courses, as well as courses in photography, ceramics, and sculpture. Many other students engage in the performing arts by taking drama courses, vocal and instrumental music lessons in various instruments of their choosing, by singing in a capella groups, and by participating in a wide variety of theatrical and musical performance opportunities. With these expert-taught, hands-on curricular and cocurricular experiences, many of these students often go on to study in universities throughout the United States and Europe, and some become practicing professional artists.[48]

Finally, while the buildings and facilities at these schools are impressive and inspiring, they seem even more advantaged being situated in beautiful locations. For many of these schools, "the affluence that serves as a backdrop to the education includes the fields, mountains, streams, lakes, deserts, swamps, and valleys owned by the schools."[49]

Social Capital

"Because we know that *where* individuals go to school determines *with whom* they associate" is a clear example of social capital.[50] "The central premise of social capital is that social networks have lasting value. Social capital refers to the collective value of all 'social networks' [whom people know] and the inclinations that arise from these networks to do things for each other ['norms of reciprocity']."[51] While it is rarely a stated reason to apply to these schools, it is certainly a well-understood benefit that one of the undeniable gains that accompanies an independent or international school diploma is membership in that school's alumni social network.

[46] www.acs.gr.
[47] http://www.kingsacademy.edu.jo/academics/departments-and-courses/fine-and-performing-arts.
[48] www.acs.gr.
[49] Cookson and Hodges-Persell, *Preparing for Power*, 48.
[50] Ibid., 16.
[51] www.bettertogether.org/socialcapital.htm.

In this way, parents not only introduce their children to these elite social networks, but they do it in an accelerated way, positioning them early to have close personal contacts within influential circles that, they hope, will provide both protection from hardship and relational channels to a better life. According to Cookson and Hodges-Pursell, "Friendships in prep schools can be deep and lasting, carrying over into adult life. Thus the web of affiliation that begins in the dormitories, on the playing fields, and in the classrooms and dining halls of elite schools does not end on the day of graduation but continues to grow, becoming more interwoven, entangled, and in the end, the basis of status group and class identity."[52]

The concept of social capital implies deliberately immersing young adolescents—such as Michaela, whom we met in the introduction—in this privileged environment that encourages influential peer relationships and educates them in associated conventions that have the potential to shape the very nature of their personal and professional networks for the future. The old adage "It's who you know," is an example of social capital, and with its implied "norms of reciprocity," may be considered part of the glue that holds group members—of various ages and stages of life—together.[53] Graduates of these schools support and appreciate each other and, at times, call on each other when they're in need. From this perspective, it is clear that an admission to one of these schools at age fourteen has the potential to influence one's life for decades to come.

Financial Strength and Stability

Underlying the stunning facilities and extensive academic and extracurricular program offerings is an abundance of money. With substantial endowments of many millions of dollars, many of these schools certainly reflect "an elite alternative to the public educational system."[54] Further, the higher the endowment, the more protected the school is from financial crises and, therefore, the more financially stable it is over decades, if not over centuries. Typically, a certain percentage of the endowment's annual earnings are reinvested to augment the endowment and to compensate

---

[52] Cookson and Hodges-Persell, *Preparing for Power*, 20–21.
[53] http://web.worldbank.org/WBSITE/EXTERNAL/TOPICS/EXTSOCIAL DEVELOPMENT/EXTTSOCIALCAPITAL.
[54] Cookson and Hodges-Percell, *Preparing for Power*, 15.

for inflation and protect against recessions in future years.[55] Since the tuition at many of these schools ranges from a low of $20,000 to a high of $58,000—where some tuitions exceed the median household income in America, which hovers around $52,000[56]—it is obviously only the wealthy who can afford these schools. That said, and part of what adds to the appeal of these schools, most of them remain so committed to enrolling qualified students—regardless of their families' financial circumstances—that they offer scholarships and generous financial aid packages to many students whose parents are unable to pay the high tuitions.

In a related way, some affluent-area public schools include per-pupil expenditures of between $20,000 and $28, 000 as part of their districts' annual budgets[57]—up to four times the national average per-pupil expenditures of just under $7000. Because of this wealth, due largely to the substantial revenues these districts collect from high property taxes in those areas, *these* public schools not only have more access to exceptional academic and instructional resources as well as state-of-the-art facilities, but they also tend to operate in very similar ways to many high-priced independent and international schools. Further, since many of the parents in these school districts tend to be both wealthy and highly educated, the students in these schools are frequently subject to the same expectations to "make the grade" and to attend the most selective colleges, just like many of their parents and teachers did.

Improved College Admissions

Without a doubt, one of the most appealing aspects of high-performance secondary schools is their individualized college application process, and their well-established track records of helping many students gain admission to selective colleges. Many schools boast that the colleges most attended by their graduates are Harvard, Columbia, Georgetown, University of Pennsylvania, Yale, Dartmouth, Amherst, Stanford, Brown, Northwestern, Middlebury, Boston College, Washington University, Cornell, Princeton, Bates, Bowdoin, Williams, Colgate, Trinity, Tufts, Pomona, Claremont McKenna, Scripps, Harvey Mudd and Pitzer. To be sure, these reports

---

[55] *So Nicely Endowed!* Newsweek: Kaplan College Guide.

[56] https://www.google.com/webhp?sourceid=chrome-instant&ion=1&espv=2&ie=UTF-8#q=median+household+income+2014.

[57] http://247wallst.com/special-report/2015/09/25/richest-and-poorest-school-districts/2/.

are very enticing, as they promote and reinforce the idea that attending a selective secondary school increases the likelihood of being admitted to a similarly selective college.

Illusion of Invulnerability

Another enticing feature of attending an independent or international school is one we can name but can't fully measure: an illusion of invulnerability. The combination of academic excellence, access to resources, and protracted social capital—all backed by considerable financial stability—frequently leads many parents to an unstated assumption that these privileged academic and social communities will enrich their children's lives and buffer them from hardship for years to come. While it is, officially, the eighth- and ninth-grade teenagers who actually apply, it is often their parents who initiate, encourage, and, ultimately, drive those applications. In this way, parents are investing in their children's immediate and long-term future. These schools know this and market their product accordingly. For example, many schools advertise their notable alumni as a way of saying, "If you come here, you, too, could be this successful." What parents wouldn't want this for their children? Among the many thousands of alumni are famous actors, authors, Nobel laureates, CEOs, diplomats, and even US presidents and foreign monarchs. These are not the careers of the needy.

Another selling point that adds to the illusion of invulnerability is that these schools promote themselves as intimate communities in which students develop in well-rounded ways: intellectually, artistically, athletically, and morally. Further, these are schools where intelligent students from many US states and foreign countries study closely with dedicated faculty members who are also their coaches, advisors, dorm parents, and, many times, their mentors. How could a teenager experience anything but contentment in such a stimulating and idyllic place?

At What Cost?

With all these advantages, it would seem that these schools do, indeed, reflect "island paradises within the larger educational system,"[58] extraordinary milieus separated from the educational mainstream designed to

---

[58] Cookson and Hodges-Percell, *Preparing for Power*, 48.

educate, shape, and mold their students, to position them for success and to provide them with a "passport to a better life."

Remember that this is how many of these schools are advertised. As in all effective advertising, these schools display their most appealing features with the intention of trying to sell their ideal educational product. They want their potential applicants to imagine themselves, or in the case of the applicants' parents, to imagine their children as "living the dream" that these schools are marketing. The question we have to ask, then, is this: "Is it really like this? Are these schools really so extraordinary?" Well ... yes! For all the reasons stated above, these schools *are* positively extraordinary. However, as my hundreds of interviews from schools around the world suggest, that isn't the whole story.

As "positively extraordinary" as these schools truly are, as institutions managed by human beings, they still have limitations. In the same way that "no one is perfect"—that as human beings, every single one of us possesses a mixture of strengths and weaknesses—no school, or any institution, for that matter, is perfect either. All schools have strengths and weaknesses, and from that human perspective, they should not expect themselves to be perfect. Like all institutions, it is not only important, but healthy, for schools to recognize and acknowledge their weaknesses and try to address them.

In "fiercely competitive schools," however, educators are reluctant to acknowledge their weaknesses and vulnerabilities. As mentioned in the introduction to this book, in an effort to remain competitive, too many educators (and parents) have unwittingly adopted a mindset that for their students, "only the best will do—in grades, test scores, sports, art, college ... in everything,"[59] as if students' perfection were actually possible. This mindset of educating for students' perfection—or as Matt Richtel termed it, "for across the board greatness"[60]—instead of educating for students' realistic sense of success, has spun out of control, out of balance. While it is understandable that educators feel that pushing their students toward reaching their potential is a strength, when that pushing leads to adverse learning conditions and to students' compromised health, it becomes a weakness. Denying this weakness can be dangerous. With this in mind, when we look past the idyllic viewbooks and websites of many elite

---

[59] Richtel, "Push, Don't Crush, the Students."
[60] Ibid.

secondary schools, and look—and listen—inside of these schools' gated walls, we see—and hear—a more complete story.

In a 2015 *Atlantic* article, "**High-Stress High School**: What's the balance between preparing students for college and ensuring they aren't killing themselves in the process?" journalist Alexandra Ossola noted, "Kids who go to elite private high schools enjoy lots of advantages ... and yet the rigor that these opportunities demand can come with extra cost for the students themselves."[61] Ossola reviewed a study from 2009 that combined qualitative interviews with faculty and staff members from a number of highly competitive private secondary schools with anonymous quantitative surveys completed by 128 students from two of these settings. The findings of that multimethod study revealed that "nearly half (49%) of all students reported feeling a great deal of stress on a daily basis,"[62] and that "a substantial minority of participants (26%) reported symptoms of depression at a clinically significant level," [63] a rate that is "over four times the [current United States] national average of 6%"[64] for overall rates of teenage depression. In 2009, these researchers described the private schools they studied as "cultures of achievement" that upheld a "futurist orientation" in which "an unremitting focus on the future [was] not developmentally consonant or appropriate for high school students."[65] Further, these same researchers reported that "chronic stress [had] been cited as the new 'cultural currency' in highly competitive private schools where students often equated their schools' level of rigor with the amount of stress [they] experienced."[66] If 49 percent of the students surveyed in 2009 reported feeling "a great deal of stress on a daily basis" and "26% reported symptoms of depression at a clinically significant level," in light of how the "fiercely competitive" conditions have only intensified since then, what would these percentages be today? Since then, have we become any more "developmentally consonant or appropriate for high school students?"

Corroborating these 2009 findings, many students today still report

---

[61] www.theatlantic.com/education/archive/2015/10/high-stress-high-school/409735, 1–2.
[62] Leonard et al., "A multi-method exploratory study of stress, coping, and substance use among high school youth in private schools," *Frontiers in Psychology*, July 23, 2015, doi: 10.3389/fpsych.2015.01028, 5.
[63] Ibid. 6.
[64] www.theatlantic.com/education/archive/2015/10/high-stress-high-school/409735, 3.
[65] Leonard, "A multi-method exploratory study," 10–11.
[66] Ibid., 2.

how stressed they feel by the burden of constant academic, social, and emotional pressure. They feel overscheduled, sleep deprived, and, frequently, "out of gas." Some report feeling overwhelmed by what one student called the "simultaneous bombardment of demands." Further, and quite unexpectedly, particularly after having successfully met their school's rigorous admissions criteria, many students experience academic *under*achievement for the first time, and then feel confused and worried about the status of their once-imagined "passport to a better life." Sadly, under the weight of "too much pressure," some students suffer disabling degrees of anxiety and depression, conditions that, if unaddressed, can lead to dangerous emotional and behavioral outcomes.

Validating these students' complaints are countless educators' and parents' reports of related unsettling concerns. For reasons that will become clearer in the next chapter, many educators freely admit to overscheduling their students, to assigning too much work, and to not following reasonable homework guidelines. Others admit to "rewarding achievement over effort," to "placing too much emphasis on grades," to "over-focusing on the college admissions process," to "not empathizing with our students," to "adhering to old notions of academic rigor," and, generally, to "expecting their students to think and act like adults long before they actually have those skillsets." Moreover, one educator admitted, "We're not presenting a curriculum that best suits our students' developmental and personal growth needs"; another stated, "We're not offering a developmentally reasonable schedule"; and another reported, "We're not implementing developmentally appropriate practices."

Throughout the process of conducting interviews for this book, I've been struck by the realization that students, educators, and parents have essentially been saying the same thing. The students say, "We're overscheduled, and there's too much work!" The educators say, "We overschedule our students, and we assign too much work!" The parents say, "We overschedule our children and micromanage their lives!" The conclusion, as so many seem to agree, is that our students are overscheduled and overworked, and sometimes that leads to very troubling consequences. Is this what we have intended? I urge that we ask ourselves: "At what cost do we all continue to operate this way?"

CHAPTER 2
The Educators: A Trouble of Our Own

It is compelling that many educators, students, and as we shall see, parents, too, are in mutual agreement about students being "overscheduled" and having "too much work." As mentioned above, I've met with hundreds of educators from a variety of US independent schools and from numerous American and international schools in Asia and Europe. The most striking realization about these meetings and interviews has been that although all of these professionals come from different schools, different states, and even from different countries, they have all reported the same problem. While they have certainly recognized the trouble that many of their students have exhibited—their anxiety, their depression, their self-destructive behavior, etc.,—these honest and well-intended educators have also reported that they, too, are in some trouble of their own, trouble that is characterized by a discouraging and seemingly unavoidable bind.

If you are an educator, at this point, quite understandably, you may be asking, "What do you mean? What is this 'discouraging and seemingly unavoidable bind'?" Rather than simply naming it for you, I invite you to observe the exact interview questions I have asked of the hundreds of faculty members and school administrators from all around the world. As you view these specific prompts, I suspect that you, too, will come to recognize the bind, and will begin to appreciate how it is compromising the very nature of our most important work.

Engaging the *Immunity to Change*

I have utilized Dr. Robert Kegan's and Dr. Lisa Lahey's *Immunity to Change*[67] paradigm as the primary interview procedure for this book. The *Immunity to Change* is a captivating change model that regards both individual and organizational change efforts as a system of compelling and competing dynamics. On the one hand, the *Immunity to Change* solicits participants to identify specific commitments they have and want to uphold, or particular changes they want or need to make. On the other hand, it also exposes "hidden dynamics that actively (and brilliantly) *prevent* [participants] from changing because of [their] devotion to preserving [their] existing ways of making meaning."[68]

In an earlier book, *How the Way We Talk Can Change the Way We Work*,[69] Drs. Kegan and Lahey introduced a "four-column conceptual grid,"[70] or what may now be described as an early version of the *Immunity To Change* paradigm. This conceptual grid was a chart of interviewees' responses to specific questions throughout this structured interview. Further, completing the first section—the "first column"—of this grid involved listing various problems and/or "complaints" that either an individual or an organization would want to try to change or address in some way.

For my interviews, I presented my participants with the list of troubled students' manifestations that I mentioned in the introduction, and asked if students in *their* schools had exhibited troubles in these or similar ways. Not surprisingly, all my participants not only recognized these symptoms but many added other symptoms to the list. Further, I then inserted this list of symptoms in "column one" of the interview grid and asked, for the sake of this procedure, that my participants would consider these student problems as *their* complaints, as concerns *they* have about many of *their* students whom they have observed to be struggling in these various ways. Consistent with how this structured interview is designed, I then proposed that if these symptoms were to represent these administrators' and teachers' complaints, then it would be "important to pay attention to these

---

[67] Kegan and Lahey, *Immunity to Change*.
[68] Ibid., x in preface.
[69] R. Kegan and L. Lahey, *How the Way We Talk Can Change the Way We Work* (San Francisco, Jossey-Bass, 2001).
[70] Ibid., 22.

complaints"[71] because "there is untapped potential there,"[72] or thoughts and feelings that could inspire their true motivation for change. As Kegan and Lahey assert, "We would not complain about anything if we did not care about something. Beneath the surface of our complaining lies a hidden river of our caring, that which we most prize or to which we are most committed."[73] All of my participants accepted this proposed premise and agreed that these were, in fact, concerns they had about many students in their schools. From that point on, they engaged each step of the protocol with their own independent responses.*

Symptoms of Struggling Students in Your School?	1. Commitments	2. Naming the Barriers: Doing/Not Doing?	3. Hidden Commitments	4. Fears that Paralyze (See Chapter Six of At What Cost?)	
Lack of motivation Sleep deprivation Procrastination Anxiety & depression Self-harming behavior Overwhelmed Academic under-achievement Substance abuse Eating Disorders Overscheduled Pressured Excessive computer gaming Suicidal ideation and behavior	I am or we, as a school, are committed to the value or importance of	In light of these commitments, what are you actually doing or not doing that gets in the way of your just-stated commitments?	Mining the Fears: Imagine doing the opposite of the behaviors you named in the previous column. What would be the most uncomfortable, worrisome or outright scary feelings that would come up for you? Identifying Competing Commitments: In addition to being committed to (educating & parenting adolescents in healthy and balanced ways), we may ALSO be committed to ...		Adapted from © Minds at Work

Adapted Four-Column Grid from the *Immunity to Change*

*The responses in this chapter reflect those of school administrators and teachers only. After having interviewed many of these school professionals, I interviewed many parents, too, and their responses are presented later in this book.

---

[71] Ibid., 20.
[72] Ibid.
[73] Ibid.

Phase 1: "From the Language of Complaint to the Language of Commitment"[74]

Here, again, is the list of "complaints" that became the starting point of all of my interviews:

"Lack of motivation; sleep deprivation; procrastination; anxiety and depression; self-harming behaviors; overwhelmed by simultaneous bombardment of demands; academic underachievement; substance abuse; eating disorders; feeling overscheduled and expected to manage without negative effects; expectations too high; excessive computer gaming, and suicide."

In an effort to prompt these administrators and teachers to identify "the hidden river of their caring, that which they most prize or to which they are most committed,"[75] I asked them to complete the following statement:

"In light of these observed student problems, I am, or we as a school are, committed to the value or the importance of ..."

Listed below are many of the free-flowing responses from these administrators and teachers.* You can hear and feel the caring, the sincerity, and the earnestness in their spontaneous responses to this initial prompt.

*These particular responses represent just a small sample of the total number of responses I gathered over these past three years. While I have listed relatively few responses here, they reflect the sentiments of the majority of participants.

"I am or we, as a school, are committed to ..."

- presenting our students with an appropriate balance of challenge and support;
- challenging our students to intellectual and personal growth with an appropriate level of rigor;
- an authentic engagement with our students;
- meeting our students where they are;
- educating our students in healthy, safe, and balanced ways;

---

[74] Ibid., 13.
[75] Ibid., 20.

- supporting our students' mental and physical health;
- promoting a healthy school culture;
- helping our students to develop their sense of identity and self-worth;
- fostering the healthy development of students in our charge;
- facilitating students' positive self-exploration and growth;
- developing students' positive sense of self;
- providing a nurturing environment for intellectual growth;
- attending to the needs of the whole student;
- producing happy learners;
- supporting our students: if we admit them, we feel committed to supporting them;
- academic rigor in a caring and connected community;
- celebrating our students' unique talents;
- finding each student's potential ... to bringing out the best in them;
- the health and well-being of all our students.

Who wouldn't see these educators' responses as sincere and heartfelt, and as expressing the "hidden river of their caring, that which they most prize or to which they are most committed?"[76] Who wouldn't support these fundamental professional commitments? In fact, I'm willing to bet that one of the main reasons why many of us chose to be teachers, counselors, and school administrators is because, collectively, we not only "like kids," but we also feel deeply committed to guiding them, to caring for them, and to providing them with what author Joy Dryfoos calls "a safe passage" from childhood to adulthood.[77]

Having successfully completed phase 1 of the *Immunity to Change* protocol, many of my interviewees acknowledged a sense of satisfaction and contentment as they had just identified, at least in part, some of their genuine professional values and commitments. Quite frankly, if the interview was to have stopped here, it would already have been a worthwhile endeavor. Having any opportunity to clarify our fundamental values and commitments can be enormously helpful in guiding our sense of professional and personal direction.

---

[76] Ibid.

[77] J. Dryfoos, *Safe Passage: Making It through Adolescence in a Risky Society: What Parents, Schools, and Communities Can Do* (New York, Oxford University Press, 2000).

Phase 2: Naming the Barriers

For phase 2 of the interview, I resumed using the exact structure of the current *Immunity to Change* paradigm, which calls for a "fearless inventory" of actual behaviors, some of which may be either self or institution implicating, that interfere with, or get in the way of the values and commitments just identified in phase 1.[78] Thus, I asked them:

> **"In light of your commitment to 'educating students in healthy, safe and balanced ways,' for example, what are you actually doing, or not doing, in your school that gets in the way of, or that interferes with that particular commitment?"**

To this prompt, administrators and teachers reported the following responses:

- We overschedule our students; we compress too much activity into an inadequate number of days and weeks.
- We always seem to pile on more, but we're never willing to do less: there's no give, so we stretch our students too thin.
- We constantly add things to our schedule, and we never take anything away from it.
- We overfocus on college admissions … it's all about college.
- We allow the outside world of the competitive college landscape to drive our program.
- We give excessive awards that emphasize high achievement instead of recognizing students' effort.
- We assign too much homework.
- We adhere to old notions of rigor and impose too much pressure on our students.
- We label and categorize many of our nonachieving students. We describe them as having ADHD or some executive function problem … and we still enforce our own high standards as nonnegotiable.
- We model and, therefore, we normalize overscheduled behavior.
- We place too much emphasis, directly and indirectly, on grades.

---

[78] Kegan and Lahey, *Immunity to Change,* 233.

- We allow students to get in over their heads.
- We expect our students to think like adults and behave like adults before they actually have those skill sets … in fact, we actively promote a developmentally unhealthy culture.
- We praise the overachievers, and we model overachieving.

In addition to these practices that these educators *do* do, they also reported on practices that they *don't* do:

- We don't follow reasonable homework guidelines, no matter what we say.
- We're not inclined to really meet kids where they are.
- We don't empathize enough with our students.
- We don't allow for flexibility in our curricular and program demands to improve students' well-being.
- We don't compromise on academic rigor: it's our currency.
- We tell our students to get enough sleep, but we don't really allow time for that.
- We don't set developmentally appropriate policies regarding study hours and lights out.
- We don't devote enough time to advising our students.
- We don't have a shared understanding of the role that stress and anxiety play in the learning process.
- We don't find opportunities to recognize "the middle" achievers.

Unlike the earlier feelings of satisfaction and contentment after completing phase 1 of the *Immunity To Change* interview, most of the administrators and teachers now admitted to feeling uncomfortable not only for having thought about, but also, for having identified more of what actually goes on in their schools, notwithstanding their genuine commitments to wanting to educate their students in healthy and balanced ways. As awkward as they felt, I assured them that because of their honesty and openness, they were much more likely to uncover their school's immunity to change, their underlying—and not so conscious—reasons why making real and lasting changes can be so difficult. They accepted my rationale and willingly volunteered to continue with the interview.

Phase 3: Eliciting Competing Commitments

This third phase of the *Immunity to Change* interview has two steps: mining the fears that underlie why trying to change the negative practices identified in stage two would be so difficult, and then actually naming the specific "competing commitments" that hold sway and interfere with our actual desires to change.

Through this process, rather than simply endeavoring to fix the aforementioned negative practices to which many educators admitted in phase 2, Drs. Kegan and Lahey propose that we "regard these behaviors as a precious resource," as "valuable information that can be mined to develop a more satisfying picture of what may really be happening."[79] Specifically, Kegan and Lahey consider these lists of negative and obstructive behaviors as "symptoms of something else rather than 'the thing itself.'"[80] Our goal in phase 3 is to mine these common practices further in an effort to understand why they might be occurring in the first place.

Step 1: "Mining the Fears"

To complete this first step, consistent with the *Immunity to Change* paradigm, I asked the teachers and administrators:

> **"Imagine yourselves trying to do the opposite"** of these negative practices, and to try to identify **"the most uncomfortable, worrisome or outright scary feelings that would come up"** for you.[81]

To this challenging question, the teachers' and administrators' candid responses reflected their sudden feelings of fear as they stated:

- If we didn't [overschedule, assign too much homework, reinforce overachievement, etc.] then we'd be seen as having lost our standards, and as lacking in rigor and excellence.
- If we didn't ... then we'd lose our standing as an elite school that gets kids into Ivy League colleges.

---

[79] Ibid., 34–35.
[80] Ibid., 35.
[81] Ibid., 238.

- If we didn't ... then we'd suffer in the college process. The colleges are ruling the roost!
- If we didn't ... then we would be perceived as intellectually 'soft.'
- If we didn't ... then our students wouldn't get in to good colleges, and we'd eventually lose our jobs.
- If we didn't ... then we fear that we might find out that 'maybe we've been wrong all along.'
- If we didn't ... then our reason for being would cease to exist, the value of our diploma would plummet, and no one would want to attend a school with such low academic standards.
- If we didn't ... then we would lose our market position, and we'd close due to lack of enrollment.
- If we didn't ... that would result in enrollment pressure that could close our school; I would lose my job as a head of school and my sense of professional identity.
- If we didn't ... then our school's financial stability would be at risk; we wouldn't get students into selective colleges, and our reputation would deteriorate.

In addition to their considering trying to do the opposite of practices they *do* do, they also reported their honest considerations of trying to do the opposite of practices they *don't* do:

- If we were to actually provide developmentally appropriate oversight and guidance for our students, then we would be depleted, overworked, and unhealthy, and we would not have balanced lives of our own.
- If we were to set more limits and establish more boundaries [around our students' behavior], then they wouldn't like us as much.
- If we actually tried to implement developmentally appropriate practices, we fear that we might try and fail ... we do what we're comfortable doing.
- If we did commit to a more developmentally healthy culture, we'd have to face our own shortcomings and areas where we need improvement; we'd have to face making adjustments in our program, which could have an impact on our jobs.
- If we actually gave in, and a developmentally reasonable schedule emerged, we might achieve a healthy balance for our students at

the cost of our school's distinctiveness; we might lose our edge of excellence and become a vanilla school, and who would want to come to a vanilla school?

Step 2: "Identifying Competing Commitments"

In light of these fears, when challenged with the request that they complete the following *Immunity to Change* prompt:

"In addition to being committed to educating our students in healthy, safe and balanced ways; or to fostering the healthy development of students in our charge; in light of our underlying fears, we may also be committed to ..."

... these same educators resumed their honest responding and made the following statements.

We may also be committed to:

- maintaining our reputation as an elite school;
- protecting our brand;
- not being perceived as intellectually soft;
- getting our students admitted to selective colleges;
- pleasing parents;
- justifying our high tuition;
- emphasizing achievement over effort;
- keeping our jobs;
- holding our market share;
- being robotic—to just going through the routines ... because that's how we've always done it;
- being objectified, where the students' sense of self is determined by external markers for success;
- encouraging toughness ... to developing [our students'] warrior spirit;
- and making our budget.

Behold the bind. For years and years, we have been encouraging parents to send their young adolescent children to rigorous and high-achieving secondary schools. Once they're admitted, we instill our students with hope, and we promise them challenging academics, close student-teacher relationships, and a nurturing and supportive environment—and we mean it. Further, with their admission, we extend a seemingly equitable opportunity for a diploma, itself an implied "passport to a better life." This is the parents' and students' aspiration, and it's the aspiration for which we, as overseers of these schools, have pledged our support and have dedicated our careers. However, when our young students actually enroll, against our best intentions but driven by our own fears, we overschedule, overwork, and sometimes overwhelm them. We set them up for frustration and failure when we expect them to think and act like adults long before they have actually developed those capacities. We reward high achievement over effort, and most of all, we overfocus on the college process almost from the moment they arrive. The comments of two educators help to characterize this hyperschooling culture. One said, "We're not just a Type A school, we're at Type A+ school ... we're extra-competitive and extra-ambitious about our uncompromising expectations."[82] Another stated, "We make the assumption that our students are capable of college-level work, as if we didn't know they're only in high school."[83]

And we wonder why many students struggle. Recall that many students report how stressed they feel by the burden of constant academic, social, and emotional pressure. They feel the effects of our overscheduling and overworking them, and of our expecting them to function like adults when they are *not* adults. One administrator confessed, "We often ask our students to do things we don't ask most adults to do: We hold kids to an unfair standard." As mentioned earlier, as a result of these conditions, many of our students are chronically sleep deprived, and many experience academic *under*achievement for the first time, and then worry that their once-imagined "passport to a better life" is in jeopardy. Part of why I started writing this book in the first place is that under the weight of all this pressure, some students suffer disabling degrees of anxiety and depression, conditions that can lead to dangerous behavioral manifestations.

As caring, decent, and dedicated educators, none of us wants to hurt *any* of our students. In fact, one of the main reasons why many of us committed to careers in education is that we like working with our students,

[82] Anonymous.
[83] Anonymous.

and we aspire to make a positive impact on their lives. The very idea that we may be actively contributing to our students' troubles has both emotional and moral implications.

From an emotional perspective, as noted in phase 1 in the *Immunity to Change* interview, most of the educators acknowledged their earnest commitments to presenting their students with "an appropriate balance of challenge and support," to challenging them "to intellectual and personal growth with an appropriate level of rigor," to being committed "to authentic engagement with [their] students: meeting them where they are," and, in general, "to educating [their] students in healthy, safe and balanced ways." As overseers of these schools, our deliberately doing *anything* different contradicts who we are and everything we've trained to do. Consequently, we feel disheartened and frustrated by the bind we are in.

With respect to moral implications, we have an obligation to live up to what we say we do. If we are, in fact, committed to "meeting students where they are," to "appropriate levels of rigor," and to "educating our students in healthy, safe and balanced ways," then *that* is what we're obligated to do. Further, if there are forces that we can now acknowledge as having controlling influences over our program's integrity, then we have an obligation to try to address them. My friend and colleague, Dr. Daniel Garvey, past president of Prescott College and of the American Youth Foundation, has repeatedly said, "We are responsible for the cultures *we* create." As the stewards of these environments, we must challenge ourselves to do things differently. We have a moral obligation to educate our students in ways that are not only consistent with our own commitments "to authentic engagement with our students: meeting them where they are;" but, also, in ways that are synchronized with *their* development. After all, students entrust themselves—not just their educations, but their whole developing selves—to us. We must honor that trust with greater respect for our students' developmental capacities.

CHAPTER 3

Students: The Reason We Exist!

In the last chapter, educators admitted to unintentionally overscheduling, overworking, and, in some cases, overwhelming their students with what we have already described as a form of hyperschooling,[84] so we have to ask ourselves, "What does this hyperschooling look like in their students' daily lives? How does hyperschooling affect students, and how do students manifest those effects?"

Effects of Hyperschooling

Here is a list of the most common ways in which many students around the world have responded to "hyperschooling" in maladaptive ways, thereby conveying that the complex demands on them far exceed their developmental capacities. While I identify these manifestations here, I will expound on them throughout the chapter. Individual students' stories help not only to personalize these responses, but also to illustrate the range with which students tend to present these reactions within their school environments.

1. Some students resign academically and refuse to do their schoolwork: they go "on strike."
2. Alternatively, many stay up too late, repeatedly, trying to complete their schoolwork, and become chronically sleep deprived. Some habitually sleep between three and five hours per night, over a period of two to three years.

---

[84] http://www.nebraskafamilyforum.org/2011/08/hyper-schooling-is-robbing-our-kids-of.html.

3. Some become inattentive and distractible, and even impulsive—all symptoms of ADHD—as if they actually have that disorder but had never exhibited those symptoms until they arrived to high school.

4. Some turn to alcohol, marijuana, prescription drugs, and to a variety of over-the-counter (OTC) medicines to get drunk or high … for relief from feeling pressured.

5. Some students lash out at others, sometimes by hazing, using aggression and/or social exclusion, to feel powerful and to offset their own underlying feelings of weakness and vulnerability.

6. Some students become addicted to computer gaming and, in so doing, develop complete other worlds of social connections with "friends" they've never met in person.

7. Some starve themselves into anorexia and/or develop chronic bulimic behaviors.

8. Some punch holes in walls, destroying school property and injuring their own hands.

9. Some repeatedly cut themselves, or in other ways inflict dangerous injuries on themselves.

10. Some students commit suicide.

Meet Abigail, an international school student who described having been up late most weekday nights, often until 2:00 or 3:00 a.m., working to complete her homework. Abigail is "a full IB" student, meaning that all of her courses are demanding and keep her extremely busy. At the end of her class day, Abigail attends her athletic practice, then hurries to one of her daily tutoring sessions for either math or French, and eventually gets home by about 8:00 or 9:00 p.m., only then to begin her long list of homework assignments. On this particular night, Abigail has to complete a complicated math assignment, study for a big test in "TOK" (Theory of Knowledge course), continue research for her Extended Essay course, and make flashcards so she can drill her French words for her weekly vocabulary quiz. Abigail said this was a typical night of homework for her, and that she didn't expect to get to bed until very late. Over time, this jam-packed schedule of work, work, work has taken its toll and has resulted in Abigail's feeling exhausted, experiencing frequent headaches, general irritability, and difficulty with concentration—all of which have led to a cumulative effect of making it even *more* difficult for Abigail to get her work done, and also to episodes of extreme anxiety.

Remarkably, if you were to meet Abigail in the hallway between classes, or in the school's dining hall at lunch, you wouldn't perceive the level of stress that lies just beneath the surface of her vivacious personality. Like many teens in these socially sophisticated environments, Abigail is a well-socialized adolescent who is highly skilled at concealing her exhaustion and irritability temporarily. However, as Abigail's parents readily acknowledge, Abigail's lively disposition "goes underground the minute she gets home as her social filters disappear and give way to exhaustion, stress and anxiety."

Abigail's experience is not atypical. The Mayo Clinic has published a list of the "Ten Signs Your Teen May be Stressed,"[85] and they are listed below:

1. Poor sleep
2. Frequent headaches and/or gastrointestinal problems
3. Anger outbursts
4. Lack of concentration
5. Increased levels of anxiety and/or panic episodes
6. Overeating/undereating
7. Increased sadness
8. Social withdrawal
9. Irritability
10. Lack of motivation

Beneath her lively but increasingly effortful presentation, Abigail manifests at least four of Mayo Clinic's symptoms of teen stress, and from what my years of clinical experience have taught me, Abigail is more the rule than the exception.

In a related article, "Pressure to Excel Can Create Too Much Tension for Teens," Mary Neiderberger of the *Pittsburgh Post-Gazette* reported, "As high achieving students push themselves further and further, parents, educators, counselors and physicians find themselves questioning: How much is too much?"[86] Further, in a forum for these concerned adults entitled "Striking a Balance: Helping our kids thrive, not just survive," parents and

---

[85] www.mayoclinic.com/health/stress-symptoms/SR00008_D.
[86] M. Neiderberger, "Pressure to Excel Can Create Too Much Tension for Teens, *Pittsburgh Post-Gazette*, March, 2012.

educators talked together of trying "to figure out a balancing act between pushing students hard enough to succeed but not so hard that they crack."[87] In that context, Mr. Jeff Longo, Student Assistance Program coordinator at North Allegheny High School, posed a question that is particularly relevant to this book: "Do kids need to compete in a complex world? Yes ... but at what cost? There's always a balance to be struck." Finally, in that same forum, Dr. Jonathan Pletcher, clinical director of Adolescent Medicine at Children's Hospital of Pittsburgh of UMPC said, "[I see] stressed-out kids daily and believe the root of the problem lies in the fact that teens are trying to meet expectations set by their parents, peers and society."[88] According to Dr. Pletcher, "My experience is it's quite the exception that teens are motivated themselves and not by some outside force. If it's not the parents, it's the media, community or other teens who reinforce the message that students need to compete to be the best, not just in academics but in many other areas as well."[89] As summarized by Ms. Neiderberger, "Mr. Longo and Dr. Pletcher believe that teaching teens to live a balanced lifestyle will better prepare them for college and for life than a hectic lifestyle packed beyond their capabilities."[90] Regrettably, in too many high-performance secondary schools, "teaching teens to live a balanced lifestyle" has been subjugated by "a hectic lifestyle packed beyond their capabilities."

Thirty years ago, speaking of high-performance independent schools, Cookson and Hodges-Persell wrote, "The external gentility of the schools often masks an incredibly demanding and sometimes unforgiving lifestyle;"[91] and that in many of these schools, "there are few mercies for the weak or inept."[92] Allusions such as these from 1985 suggest, at least for the past thirty years, that many of these schools have maintained—maybe even promoted—a reputation of being "incredibly demanding and sometimes unforgiving," and of being schools in which the "weak or inept" might not enlist the "mercies" of the faculty. Even thirty years ago, these schools' modus operandi seemed incongruous with what psychological research had already identified.

Approximately seventy years earlier, psychologists Robert Yerkes and

---

[87] Ibid.
[88] Ibid.
[89] Ibid.
[90] Ibid.
[91] Cookson and Hodges-Persell, *Preparing for Power*, 20.
[92] Ibid.

John Dodson (1908) studied the relationship between performance and anxiety, and devised what became known as the Yerkes Dodson law [93] proving that when *anyone*, in *any* setting, is challenged with performance demands that far exceed his or her functional capacities, debilitating anxiety ensues. Thirty years ago, schools' "incredibly demanding and sometimes unforgiving" approach may have been one of their prized distinctions, like a medal of honor worn by graduates who had survived their schools' many pressures. Today, however, particularly in light of how competitive conditions have intensified, and of what we now know about how damaging these pressured conditions can be, for these schools to *continue* to operate with "incredibly demanding and sometimes unforgiving" practices could be considered not only insensitive, but also irresponsible.

I am frequently asked, "Is this situation getting worse?" "Is the trouble intensifying?" I believe it is. Due to a variety of economic and cultural factors mentioned earlier, the competition to attend independent and international schools has intensified, as have the pressures to remain and excel there. As Ken Robinson points out, "Many countries are increasing the numbers of students who go to college. In Europe and the United States in the fifties and sixties, about one in twenty people went to college. Between 1970 and 2000, there was a global increase of almost 300 percent.[94] In the developed economies at least, about one in three high school graduates now heads for college. Getting into college is now widely seen as the ultimate purpose of high school."[95] Reinforcing these statistics, one admissions administrator recently told me, "Our applications have basically doubled in the last decade, and this increase has been equally domestic and international as the web has opened up many markets."[96]

Consider the role that international demands have had on the competition to attend independent and international schools. As mentioned earlier, in her *New York Times* article, Lucy Hornby-Reuters reported that "upwardly mobile Chinese parents are willing to pay as much as 260,000

---

[93] R. M. Yerkes and J. D. Dodson, "The relation of strength of stimulus to rapidity of habit-formation," *Journal of Comparative Neurology and Psychology* 18 (1908): 459–82.

[94] Word Bank Education Statistics, retrieved from http://datatopics.worldbank.org/education/EdstatsHome.aspx. (Cited in: K. Robinson and L. Aronica, *Creative Schools: The Grassroots Revolution That's Transforming Education* (New York, Viking, 2015), 11.

[95] K. Robinson and L. Aronica, *Creative Schools: The Grassroots Revolution That's Transforming Education* (New York, Viking, 2015), 11.

[96] Anonymous.

renminbi, or about $42,000, a year for a Western-style education and a possible ticket to a college overseas for their children,"[97] and that "the number of international schools registered in mainland China has soared in the past 12 years, to 338 from 22" because "parents who can afford the international schools say it is a passport to a better life for their children, despite much higher costs."[98]

Similarly, in a subsequent *New York Times* piece, Joyce Lau highlighted that "a century ago, international schools were small, elite replicas of Western schools for the generally white, rich children of parents posted in 'exotic' locales." However, Lau reported that "as developed nations have become wealthier and as the world has become more multicultural, international schools have boomed. According to ISC Research in Britain, there are now 6,400 international schools all over the globe. In a decade, that number is expected to almost double."[99]

Nearly ten years earlier, in 2004, *Wall Street Journal* writer Elizabeth Bernstein wrote, "Competition has intensified as the kids of baby boomers reach college age," and in a related way, "tuition at private schools—believed by many parents to be the best insurance for college admission—is soaring to record levels."[100] At that time, reported Bernstein, "tuition of $20,000 a year [was] routine, with several of the best-known private schools topping $25,000."[101] In only a decade, tuition at most of the "best-known private schools" has more than doubled. To be sure, many parents are still willing to pay for what they hope will be "the best insurance for college admission," or as we've already seen, for a "passport to a better life for their children."

Complicating matters is the fact that competition for the most selective colleges has also intensified, a phenomenon whose trickle-down effect has only increased competition to attend high-achieving secondary schools. In another *New York Times* article, "Best, Brightest and Rejected: Elite Colleges Turn Away Up to 95%," Richard Perez-Pena reported, "Enrollment at American colleges is sliding, but competition for spots at top universities is more cutthroat and anxiety-inducing than ever. In the [2014] admissions season, Stanford University accepted only 5 percent of applicants, a [then current] new low among the most prestigious schools, with the odds nearly

---

[97] Hornby-Reuters, "International Schools in China."
[98] Ibid.
[99] Lau, "International Schools Boom."
[100] E. Bernstein, "The Price of Admission," *Wall Street Journal*, April 2, 2004, W1.
[101] Ibid.

as bad at its elite rivals."[102] Recall that in the most recent 2016 admissions season, Stanford reported "an ultra-low admit rate of 4.7%."[103] Perez-Pena further noted, "Deluged by more applications than ever, the most selective colleges are, inevitably, rejecting a vast majority, including legions of students they once would have accepted. Admissions directors at these institutions say that most of the students they turn down are such strong candidates that many are indistinguishable from those who get in."[104]

One of the major effects of all this pressure is that as the college competition intensifies, our younger students compete even more with each other to the extent that, ironically, everyone starts to look alike. They all have very high SAT scores; they all have numerous AP courses or, for international school students, have completed "the full IB"; they all have very high academic averages as well as multiple extracurriculars, numerous awards, and outstanding achievements. This "across-the-board greatness"[105] reflects a sense of sameness that turns out to be the very heart of the problem for our students. Their untiring search for identity—itself a hardwired, developmentally determined effort to "distinguish" themselves as unique among their peers—gets hijacked by this increasingly competitive culture. Thus, for any student to know that he or she might be perceived as "indistinguishable" can be both a cause for disillusionment, and a threat to the very code by which they are developmentally hardwired to live and to make meaning in their teenage years.

For another example, meet Devlin, a recent independent school graduate who recalls his own experience of his school's fiercely competitive environment.

> I was involved with a lot of different activities ... sports, theater, student government and several clubs. A lot of my friends did these things, too. It was like we all felt this sense of competition, some of which we put on ourselves, but some of it came from the school. Basically, we went through school, having heard from like freshman year on, that we should do as much as possible to build up our

[102] http://www.nytimes.com/2014/04/09/us/led-by-stanfords-5-top-colleges-acceptance-rates-hit-new-lows.html?_r=0.
[103] www.washingtonpost.com/news/grade-point/wp/2016/04/05/stanford-dean-schools-ultra-low-admit-rate-not-something-to-boast-about/.
[104] Ibid.
[105] Richtel, "Push, Don't Crush."

resumes for our college applications. Actually, I remember thinking about that in the 8th grade, which was one of the reasons I even applied to this school. I remember thinking, "If I go to [school name], then I'll have a better chance of getting in to a good college."

Anyway, in the fall of junior year, we had this all-class meeting about how to start the college process. While I had been expecting that meeting, it still made me nervous. Even though we wouldn't actually be applying to college until the next year, there was something about having the whole process kick in an entire year earlier. I think everyone was like, "Oh my god ... here we go." It was like a big anxiety shift for the whole class. I remember thinking, "Are my grades good enough? Will I do well on the SATs? Have I done enough extracurricular activities? Should I do more? Should I take another AP course? Do I even have a chance of getting in to the colleges I've imagined applying to?"

I think that's when the competition really started to build. Suddenly, kids were like trying to get captain of their sports teams, or were trying to start new clubs just so they could be the leader of them, so they could say that on their resumes. It just seemed that more and more kids were suddenly competing for leadership positions ... not so much because they were interested in them, but because they felt they needed them for their resumes. It was really stressful because in such a small school, there weren't really enough leadership opportunities to go around ... and everyone wanted to lead something.

The psychologically threatening nature of the competitive college process has been well documented. According to Lucy Hart of Demand Media, "The college admissions process can induce feelings of inferiority in students [as it] forces [them] to deal with unwanted advice, shame or invasion of privacy brought on by external influences, such as high school administration, admissions boards and their peers."[106] As many of today's

[106] http://everydaylife.globalpost.com/college-admission-requirements-negatively-affecting-students-16932.html.

college applicants can attest, the whole process can result in their "doubting themselves and their capabilities, negatively affecting their self-esteem."[107] Alarmingly, as noted recently by columnist Frank Bruni, "For too many parents and their children, acceptance by an elite institution isn't just another challenge, another goal. A yes or a no from [an elite college or university] is seen as the conclusive measure of a young person's worth, an uncontestable harbinger of the accomplishments or disappointments to come. Winner or loser: This is when the judgment is made. This is the great, brutal culling."[108] Not surprisingly, under such fiercely pressured and competitive conditions, many students "become consumed with the 'survival of the fittest' mentality, which negatively affects the quality of their [overall] high school experience."[109]

As many educators have already revealed, those educators in high-achieving secondary schools are not only aware of this phenomenon, but they seem to have accepted and internalized it, responding in their own pressured way by overscheduling and overworking students in *their own* efforts to remain competitive. As a result of these collective responses, many high-achieving students confront three realities: (1) schools tend to "overschedule and overwork" their students; (2) high-achieving schools around the world are in competition with each other, all trying to recruit "the best and brightest" students to enroll at *their* schools; and (3) each school strives to advance *its own* students to any one of a tiny cluster of the world's most selective colleges. Because of these combined realities, an increasingly competitive "eye of the needle" effect has emerged as more and more qualified students from a growing number of schools around the world vie for the same very-few acceptances at the world's most selective colleges. Consequently, these extremely competitive conditions trickle down to secondary schools and generate similarly extreme pressures that reinforce and feed on each other, rendering *all* our students feeling caught in an intensified pressure vortex. Indeed, while some students withstand these pressures more effectively than others, most students experience them. Regrettably, these intense pressures accumulate, and in a variety of

---

[107] Ibid.

[108] F. Bruni, "How to Survive the College Admissions Madness," *New York Times*, March 13, 2015.

[109] http://everydaylife.globalpost.com/college-admission-requirements-negatively-affecting-students-16932.html.

direct and indirect ways, inflict the most harm on the most developmentally vulnerable individuals, students.

Perhaps Cookson and Hodges-Persell said it best: "students are taught that they should be moral and treat life as an exciting challenge, but what they often learn is that life is hard, and that winning is essential for survival."[110] Further, "Pressure on these students is relentless. From the moment they jump over (or stumble through) the hurdles of admission to [their school], they must prove their worth by mastering the curriculum, the student culture, and their own vulnerability. The pressure to get into the right college can be excruciating for many of these young people. While they are taught cooperation, they learn competition. And they also have to grow up quickly: 'Adolescent problems aren't real,' one dean said with chilling finality. We began to see [elite] schools as crucibles from which some students emerge as tempered steel and others were simply burnt to a crisp."[111]

It is compelling that Cookson and Hodges-Persell saw these high-performance schools "as crucibles" when they wrote their book thirty years ago, when the admissions rates at the most selective colleges hovered around the 20 percent rate,[112] compared to today's rates of between 5 and 6 percent.[113] Considering the fierce competition that has developed since the mid-1980s, if these schools were "crucibles" then, have they become "the fire" now? In an effort to keep pace with this competitive trend, how many schools have gone from being "the frying pan" of the 1980s to "the fire" of the twenty-first century? How has this "heating up" affected the students? While the "tempered steel" students may have survived the schools' steadily intensifying heat, what has it cost them to do so? One of my colleagues often states, "We want our students to thrive, not just survive!"[114] After being "tempered," are our students emotionally, behaviorally, and socially fit? Most importantly, what developmental costs have our students paid in their efforts to survive their schools' "incredibly demanding and sometimes unforgiving lifestyle?" From my vantage point, the primary

---

[110] Cookson and Hodges-Persell, *Preparing for Power*, 19.

[111] Ibid., 20.

[112] oir.yale.edu/node/57/attachment (Yale University Office of Undergraduate Admissions October Report. OIR W033. Freshmen Admissions Summary [01/15/14]).

[113] http://www.nytimes.com/2014/04/09/us/led-by-stanfords-5-top-colleges-acceptance-rates-hit-new-lows.html?_r=0.

[114] David Rost, former dean of students, Concord Academy, Concord, Massachusetts.

cost of students' trying to survive their schools' "heat" is that they are increasingly deprived of "being adolescent" because they're so busy, if not harried, trying desperately to be "adults" and to meet expectations that exceed their capabilities.

Recall that in my many interviews, educators admitted openly that they "overwork their students" and "expect students to act like adults and think like adults before they even have those capacities." Laura, a graduate of a high-achieving international school, recalled her experiences of struggling to manage how overworked she felt.

> I was taking five IB courses; I was president of Debating Club, and had a lot of event planning for that. I was also one of the leads in the school play ... all at the same time ... and I knew I needed these things because I wanted to put them on my resume for my applications because I felt like I was lacking. I only got around 4-5 hours of sleep most nights. My day-to-day schedule would be like ... right after school I'd have meetings for the Debate Club, I'd go to play rehearsal right after that, then I'd go my tutor's house where she would review my applications work ... and then I'd go home and do my homework at about 8-9 pm. My family hardly ever saw me for dinner. I would often eat at my tutor's house. My mom caught me crying a lot. I cried a lot because I didn't think I could do it. I always felt like there was too much on my plate ... and I was worried that something was always about to fall.
>
> Sometimes I did all-nighters. Doing all-nighters was a huge thing for everybody. I remember one of these nights ... it was around 5 am ... and the sun was coming up ... and I was dying to sleep but I couldn't because I had to finish my work ... and then the tears came out. My mom could hear me ... my crying would wake her up ... that was bad. So I guess in general, my personality was changing; my diet was changing; I was gaining weight; I was looking different. I was just so stressed out.

Mark, a current independent school student and a senior dorm prefect, recalled a dorm situation in which he felt unprepared to deal with the seriousness of the issue. As Mark reported, "I felt like I had to be like a trained therapist."

> There was this kid in my dorm who had just learned that his parents were getting a divorce. I knew the kid pretty well, and I knew he was devastated. Anyway, my dorm parent asked me to check in on this kid and to try to talk to him about it ... but it was kind of heavy stuff and I wasn't sure how to handle it. I did it, but I felt really awkward ... and had to pretend that I knew what I was doing. Mostly, I wondered why my dorm parent asked me to try to handle it first. As a prefect, there have been many situations in which I have felt like I've been treated like an adult. Part of me has liked that, but at the same time, it has also felt kinda strange. I've had a lot of experiences where I've had to pretend that I am more grown-up than I am.

In another example, Kim recounted her experience of having been a student-member of her school's Judicial Committee. Kim reported:

> As a junior, I applied to be one of the student reps on the JC but I had no idea then that it would be so stressful. Judging your friends, listening to adults judge your friends, and sometimes, getting blamed by these friends if the JC doesn't turn out the way they want it ... it's all just really stressful. I had this really awkward situation when one of my good friends had to go before the JC for an alcohol violation, and I was one of the student reps in that meeting. This friend pressured me to advocate for her, but I knew she had lied to the JC. It was really awkward because I knew she had lied, but I didn't want to be the one to expose her to the rest of the group. Thankfully, the faculty members sensed the lie, too, so they brought it up ... and I didn't have to be the one to tell on her. It was still really stressful, and that situation totally changed my friendship with that kid. I'm still angry that she put me in that position.

Rick, another international school student, described his recent experience of feeling inept in his role as a team captain.

> There were definitely times when my coach seemed to put too much stock in my power as a captain and what he thought I could manage ... and there were times when I felt pressure about what he was asking me to do. I know I was captain of his team, but I often thought I was asked to do more than I felt comfortable doing. It just seems that adults at this school often treat us like we're adults, too, and sometimes it feels like we're being asked to take on more than we should.

Devlin, Laura, Mark, Kim, and Rick were articulate about not feeling able or ready to fulfill the "adult" roles into which they felt cast. From a developmental perspective, these students' feelings are perfectly valid. Psychologist Robert Kegan writes poignantly about one of the most common developmental errors adults make in their interactions and dealings with adolescents.[115] Since adolescents develop physically in ways that resemble fully grown adults, and since adolescents also begin to speak and move with the sophistication we associate more with adults than with children, it is very common for adults to be misled by adolescents' adult-like appearance and composure, and to then treat those adolescents *as if they were* adults. Kegan warns, however, that "if adults mistake [adolescents'] physiology and/or [their] verbal ability for [their] psychological age,"[116] and then expect those adolescents to function as if they're actually young adults, then it's the adults who "create a situation which is dangerous for both themselves and for the developmentally delayed teenager."[117] As Kegan asserts, "The cost to a person of being unseen, of being seen as the person-one-might-become rather than the person-one-is,"[118] is a "bewildering experience of being unfairly demanded of."[119]

In these increasingly competitive schools, and at an increasingly disturbing rate, students are "being unseen" for who they actually are

---

[115] R. Kegan, *The Evolving Self* (Cambridge, MA: Harvard University Press, 1982), 178.
[116] Ibid.
[117] Ibid.
[118] Ibid.
[119] Ibid., 179.

and, instead, are being seen as "persons-they-might-become." For many students, this is, indeed, a "bewildering experience of being unfairly demanded of." While schools are certainly charged with the mission of educating their students, they are also charged with being places in which students can develop friendships and learn to get along with one another, where they can take appropriate academic and social risks, where they can experience success and develop self-confidence, and where they can also experience setbacks but learn how to manage and grow from them. Essentially, in addition to schools being places in which children and adolescents learn academically, schools are also places in which children and adolescents learn socially and emotionally. Schools are places in which children and adolescents do much of their growing up. From this perspective then, schools, along with families and peers, are major contributors to what pediatrician and psychoanalyst D. W. Winnicott termed a child's "holding environment," or the collective surround of the people, places, and experiences that make up a child's social world.[120]

Subsequent to Winnicott's work, Robert Kegan, in his seminal book about constructive-developmental theory, asserted that holding environments extend throughout the human lifespan. Further, Kegan theorized that holding environments are not simply passive settings in which children have their experiences, but that they are active milieus in which the key adults who constitute them serve essential developmental functions.[121] Not surprisingly, the most important function of any holding environment, at any age or stage of development, is to "hold," or in Kegan's terms, to "confirm and recognize the individual's unique developmental integrity."[122] For our purposes, "well-held" students within our schools' holding environments would be those students who feel "confirmed and recognized" for their "unique developmental integrity," instead of "being unseen," and therefore, unknown and misunderstood.

Kegan's assertion that when adolescents are "unseen ... [it] creates a situation which is dangerous for both [the adults] and for the developmentally delayed teenager" is exactly right. In fact, these are the "dangerous situations" I have been observing and treating for two decades. Not surprisingly, many students feel flattered, initially, by their teachers' and

---

[120] D. W. Winnicott, *The Maturational Processes and the Facilitating Environment* (London: Hogarth Press, 1976).

[121] Kegan, *The Evolving Self*, 121.

[122] Ibid.

parents' "adult-like" demands. "They have confidence in me!" and "They think I can do it!" are common early perceptions of our motivated and eager-to-please students. However, these complimentary feelings quickly fade and often turn into frustration, anger, guilt, and shame as many of these same students eventually realize they cannot live up to those too-high expectations, that they cannot sustain an "adult-like" level of functioning because, quite simply, they are not adults, as "they haven't even developed those capacities yet."

As we have already seen, however, for some students the adult-like pressures not only remain, but intensify. As one student recently told me, "Sometimes, the pressure is immense!" Consequently, as these students feel "unseen" by their educators and parents, they feel frustrated and try to cope by struggling even more to live up to the adults' expectations. Further, if these students have not developed direct ways of expressing their pressured feelings with words—skills many adults haven't developed, either—then they usually find indirect ways of expressing themselves. Many of them act out their feelings, as if to cry out, "How far do I have to push this before my (teachers, parents, coaches, etc.) hear me ... before they actually do something to help me with all this pressure?"

The term "acting out" refers to a psychological phenomenon in which individuals "act out" feelings that are otherwise too difficult—too powerful, too scary, too shameful—to express with words. Slamming a door, swearing, or hitting another person are common examples of how individuals sometimes act out feelings of anger. Cutting and other forms of self-injury are common behaviors that express extreme anxiety and depression. In these high-stress moments, intense emotional pain overpowers rational thinking and gives way to aggressive, defensive and/or temporarily self-soothing behavior, often with lingering negative consequences. While acting out behaviors are usually destructive, either to oneself or to others, nevertheless, they often help to establish balance once again, a return to a brief emotional equilibrium as they relieve the individual of immediate and prevailing distress.

Here are a few students who have resorted to indirect expressions of the pressure associated with "situations which [are] dangerous for both [the adults] and for the developmentally delayed teenagers."

Matthew, an independent school junior, experienced chronic depression.

"At the start of sophomore year, I started to hate my life here. I hated everything ... my schedule, my homework, my friends ... and myself. I remember thinking, 'I suck,' and 'I'm not smart enough to be at this school ... whatever I do, it's never enough.'"

Matthew had earned mostly Bs throughout his freshman year—which was good—but from his perspective, one that he had fully internalized, "mostly Bs" wasn't good enough. Matthew had already come to believe that no matter what he did, he just couldn't measure up to his teachers,' his parents', or his own expectations.

"My parents went to great colleges, and they're totally invested what college I go to, too. What if I don't get in to a good college? With getting only Bs, I definitely won't get into a good college, and that just makes me feel worse." In one session, Matthew reported, "I don't want to do anything in this school anymore. I haven't done homework for about two weeks; all I do is sleep all the time or just get on my computer and do nothing ... wasting time. I think I stopped caring about school a long time ago, and I have no motivation at all."

As a freshman, Matthew had felt more engaged and competitive with his peers. Since then, however, under the pressure of trying to keep up, Matthew has lost more and more motivation, which eroded the sense of buoyancy with which he had confidently applied to this school as an eighth-grader.

"Those awful feelings [of depression] are really, really scary. I have no joy in my life anymore, so why live? I think about killing myself all the time."

Philippe, a recent graduate of an international school, recalls the role of alcohol among his peers.

> I saw that everyone seemed angry all the time ... because they were so scared and stressed ... and it seemed like that for the whole senior year. But in this country, you can drink at 18, so on weekends, kids would go a little harder ... like there'd be this whole bunch of kids going out to relieve stress ... or at least trying to ... under the influence of alcohol. They'd drink to try to have fun with their friends because back at school, everyone was too pressured, too scared and too competitive with each other. Everyone would come to school on school days upset ... but they drank a lot together during the weekends to try to help.

Mackenzie struggles with an eating disorder.

Mackenzie reports that since she has been at her new school, she has questioned her own intelligence, and therefore, her value as a person. For Mackenzie, feeling like she can't control being "bombarded with demands," she has tried to compensate by controlling her weight, itself a distorted and superficial, but to her, guaranteed way of maintaining "visible proof of my self-worth." Mackenzie admits to having felt "attractive" at times, a feeling she craves, but a feeling that also leads to added pressure. Even a slight change in body weight triggers intense feelings of self-hatred and self-loathing. As Mackenzie states, "Sometimes I cry at the thought of eating ... each meal is a huge ordeal ... I hate food." Further, Mackenzie admits, "I have this vision that once I'm skinnier, things will get better. I'll run faster; I'll test better and get better grades; I'll have more friends; I'll be more confident ... and life will get a lot easier."

For the record, by normal growth and development charts, Mackenzie is already below her recommended healthy weight. The longer Mackenzie resists food, the more anorexic she becomes, and the more she endangers herself. For Mackenzie, poor nutrition compromises not only her physical health, but also her cognitive development and her education itself—the very reason she came to this school in the first place. Tragically, in Mackenzie's mind, controlling food intake is a sure way to "make myself skinny" (which to her means "valuable, smarter, faster, confident ..."), as she tries desperately to compensate for the self-worth injuries that began with her anxiety about not feeling smart enough amid her school's demanding curriculum and culture.

Keara admits to both alcohol use and self-injury.

Keara, a senior, after a few months of weekly counseling sessions, finally trusts me enough to say, "You know how we talked about the times I scratched myself ... and drank just enough to numb my feelings but not enough to get sick or caught?"

"Yes."

"Well ... I might have made those things seem a little better than they were."

For the next several minutes, Keara admits to having cut herself "about two to three times a week ... on [her] hips where it doesn't show." She admits to having scars there, too, but she also states, "They're not too bad ... they'll heal."

Keara is beginning to recognize her own pattern of "a slow buildup of stress and tension," a pattern she doesn't really feel until it's too late ... when she acts out by cutting herself. Keara admits to having learned, over time, to just "take it," and to "hold [her] feelings in." Now, however, she is beginning to acknowledge the self-destructive costs of having tried to "take it" and "hold her feelings in."

Like many others, Keara manages the many pressures by turning to alcohol use to "numb [her] feelings," and also by cutting herself, as both behaviors have helped her to either avoid or release the tension that she claims "builds up to an intolerable level." As Keara states, "Drinking and cutting work ... in the short term." Sadly, Keara's pattern of drinking and self-injury also reinforce her recurrent feelings of disgrace and shame for repeatedly falling back on these addictive and maladaptive coping behaviors.

"It's so weird," Keara reports, "I can talk about it now—after the fact— but I can't talk about these things when I'm feeling that way. At those times, I just need to *do* something ... and that's when I drink or cut ... they relieve the pressure."

Suicide

Note: I have known too many schools that have dealt with one or more of their students who have committed suicide. Rather than mention any of these cases specifically, in an effort not to drag these schools through that psychological pain—they would recognize themselves in this book, and that seems both unnecessary and unfair—I have generalized here.

Sadly, many students from high-performance schools around the world have died by suicide. Some students have committed suicide to escape increasing feelings of humiliation about not being able to meet the academic demands with which they have been confronted. Some have committed suicide in response to feeling intense shame as a consequence of school-related disciplinary situations. Still others have committed suicide to end relentless feelings of anxiety and depression that have not only persisted, but that have overwhelmed their abilities to cope. While the specific triggers for these students' suicides have varied—although there have been predicable patterns there, too—the underlying cause of most of these tragic deaths has essentially been the same. For each of these students, the accumulation of pressures—whatever their origin—has overpowered their available coping skills. In their youthful shortsightedness, feeling helpless and desperate, these students have resorted to extreme and irreversible solutions to understandable, if not preventable, short-term problems.

Fundamentally, the question, "At what cost?"—the social, emotional, and developmental costs—is a multifaceted one, and it's a question I have asked rather frequently. I am often in meetings to review a particular student's status—usually after some academic or social-emotional crisis—during which key administrators and the student's advisor and parents join forces to discuss the student's current standing at the school. Inevitably, discussing the student's recently exposed vulnerabilities leads to further discussion of whether or not the challenges of the school outweigh the supports available there. Not uncommonly, I ask those assembled to consider the question, "At what cost are we expecting this student to be at this school?"

In truth, in order to answer this question comprehensively, we must first examine the developmental landscape of *all* early adolescents. Given recent and unprecedented advances in neuroimaging, as well as findings from associated research in the fields of child development, neuropsychology, and health care, we *all* need an updated, age-related baseline understanding. Who are these kids, really, whom we admit to our schools and claim to understand? What pressures are these kids actually encountering when they enroll in these rigorous schools? How much pressure is okay? How can we distinguish between enough and too-much pressure? How does too-much pressure affect our students?

In the next section, we explore an array of developmental and environmental pressures that, when combined—as they are for *all* our students—provide a broad perspective not only of our students' developmental readiness, but also, of their actual capacities to meet our schools' demands.

PART 2

Pressures, Neurodevelopment, and Costs

CHAPTER 4

Under Pressure

Many high school students experience numerous and overlapping pressures that, if overlooked, can be troublesome. For example, many students feel enormous pressure to "make the grade," or to measure up to intense expectations for academic and extracurricular excellence. Driven by both internal and external pressures, most of these students lead highly demanding, if not frenetic, lives as they take advanced courses, play sports three seasons each year, participate in drama productions, take music lessons, participate in community service, and stay up too late many nights trying to complete their homework assignments. One student remarked, "The school day isn't just till three in the afternoon ... it goes until at least midnight or later. I always feel overwhelmed. On any given day, I have a full day of classes, maybe a of couple tests, then I usually have a club meeting, then I have to run to sports practice, and after practice, run to dinner ... then to a choir rehearsal ... this is a normal day ... then I commute home by like nine thirty or ten and *then*, I have to start my homework ... then get ready to do it all over again. This past year, I was up really late almost every night ... until like one or one thirty in the morning ... just to get my work done."

As this student illustrates, inevitable feelings of stress emerge when students realize they can't do it all, but feel compelled to try anyway. Unfortunately, many who try to "do it all" do so with significant costs. For example, another student remarked, "It's common knowledge that there are these four balls at this school, and you can only keep three of them in the air. They're called the four *S*'s: school, sleep, social life, and sports, and you *have* to choose which one's going to fall." As this student explains, try as they might, managing "the four *S*'s" can be a daunting, if not overwhelming, challenge.

Why do so many of these students put so much pressure on themselves? Where does this pressure come from? As suggested above, some of these pressures are "internal," as these seem to come from within, while other pressures are "external," pressures that are imposed on students by a variety of environmental sources. Most importantly, for many students, these pressures are combined and simultaneous, and, therefore, they emerge as cumulative feelings of overwhelming pressure. In this section, we explore numerous areas from which these pressures originate, combine, and, in some circumstances, give way to troublesome manifestations.

Nature: Pressure from Within

For all children, the onset of puberty triggers a succession of physical and psychological changes, including the capacity to think more abstractly, well beyond the concrete boundaries of the early years. Psychologist and theorist Jean Piaget termed this the Formal Operations stage of cognitive development, as he claimed that early adolescents are newly capable of hypothetical reasoning, the ability to imagine possibilities, develop hypotheses concerning what *might* occur, to reason about *that* and to derive new, abstract interpretations.[123] Further, another psychologist and theorist, Erik Erikson, postulated that with their budding cognitive capacities, early adolescents become captivated with more personal hypothetical concerns as they begin to wonder, "Who am I?" and "What can I be?" In 1968, Erikson referred to this phase of development, Identity vs. Role Confusion, as an "end of childhood,"[124] and "a crisis of wholeness,"[125] and then asserted that for adolescents to "experience wholeness, they must feel a progressive continuity between that which has come during the long years of childhood, and that which promises to become in the anticipated future."[126] Wholeness, claims Erikson, results from an ongoing and delicate balance between what adolescents conceive themselves to be and that which they perceive others to see and expect in them.[127]

While some of these "others" are adults—parents, teachers, coaches,

---

[123] H. P. Ginsburg and S. Opper, *Piaget's Theory of Intellectual Development* (New Jersey, Prentice Hall, 1988), 206.
[124] E. H. Erikson, *Identity: Youth and Crisis* (New York, W. W. Norton, 1968), 87.
[125] Ibid.
[126] Ibid.
[127] Ibid.

etc.—many of these "others" are peers. Propelled by a developmentally determined compulsion to try on new roles and identities on the one hand, and by an equally compelling need to be acknowledged and accepted on the other, adolescents find both strength and comfort among their peers as they join various cliques, teams, and mutual interest groups. As a high school sophomore, I remember feeling a sense of belonging and pride when I received my royal-blue-with-white-leather-sleeves track team jacket. That jacket was a concrete sign of membership on my school's track team, and it temporarily fortified my still-vulnerable sense of self while I continued to experiment with other roles. Today's teenagers identify themselves in many ways: preppies, jocks, brains, emos, goths, skaters, surfers, punks, gamers, etc. Whether it's jocks wearing the same athletic shoes, goths wearing dark clothes and dark makeup, or preppies sporting Polo and J. Crew wardrobes, all of these teenagers are up to the same business. They're all experimenting with new roles and trying to take comfort in "looking the part," whatever part that may be. Generally, adolescents the world over behave and dress in ways that simultaneously express their peer group affiliation and yearn for acceptance from that same group—the seeds of identity formation and desired "wholeness"—as they ponder various roles they'll eventually assume in adulthood. Erikson underscored the significance of the adolescent drive to attain a reliable sense of identity as he wrote of adolescents' "persistent endeavor to define, over-define and redefine themselves and each other in often ruthless comparison"[128] in an effort to avoid a sense of role confusion, a condition Erikson described as "the horror of undefinedness."[129] It is a felt experience of "the horror of undefinedness" that prompts many teens to act in self-destructive ways, as they try to cope with these scary feelings.

As these historical and theoretical references convey, adolescents' striving for their own unique identities comes from within. It is a naturally determined, hardwired experience of pressure to find even a preview of their emerging identity, a basic feeling that they are "okay" and that they're recognized and validated for who they are. This neuro-developmental pressure is intended to motivate their growth, to facilitate their eventual separation from home, and ultimately, to promote their independence and autonomy for the adult world. For every adolescent, this is a matter of ultimate concern.

[128] Ibid.
[129] Ibid.

Peter Newhall, a fourteen-year-old American student living abroad with his parents, is a telling example of this internally motivated pressure. I asked Peter's parents why they would even consider sending their child overseas to boarding school. Mr. Newhall said, "We'll miss him to the point where it hurts. We love Peter, and we want to be near him, but *he* wants to do this, *he* wants to go, *he's* been the one pushing us to let him apply. At this point, Peter feels like he can really benefit from all that is so good about these schools. And I guess there's one more thing: we feel that Peter absolutely needs to get out from under our sometimes-too-careful watch if he's going to spark his own inspirations." Mr. Newhall's comments so clearly illustrate how Peter's own internal stirrings simultaneously motivate his own growth, initiate a risky separation from his parents, and, ultimately, promote his own eventual independence and autonomy for the adult world.

Nurture: Pressure Imposed by Culture and Society

For many of today's teenagers, external pressures begin well before they're even aware of them: in preschool. A 2006 *New York Times* article conveyed: "Fierce competition for private preschool in New York City [had] propelled to a frenzy by the increased numbers of children vying for scarce slots."[130] Further, a local Bright Horizons preschool boasts, "Our children are young readers, scientists, musicians, artists and explorers who are encouraged to reach their full potential," and that the faculty there "help children of all ages and stages to see the world as an invitation to learn, grow and live fully and prepare them to approach school and academics."[131] While there is little doubt that these high-priced preschools and kindergartens are staffed with caring and professional educators, what does it say about the culture in which these children are being raised? Above and beyond the high tuition costs that the parents pay, what personal and developmental costs do the children pay? As an international school teacher stated during one of my conference workshops, "Kids are under pressure to be successful *all* the time, in everything: they're trying to manage adult-like demands before they're ready." Another educator stated, "Schools reflect the pressures of the parents; schools are businesses, after all, so they must appeal to what their clientele want."

---

130 http://www.nytimes.com/2006/03/03/education.
131 http://explore.brighthorizons.com/?p=Preschool.

The 2010 documentary film *Race to Nowhere* reinforces these themes and features students, parents, educators, and psychologists who "challenge current thinking about how we prepare our children for success."[132] One student remarks, "School is just so much pressure that everyday I'd wake up dreading it." Another student is filmed stating, "Everyone expects us to be superheroes!" Further, a teacher states, "Our students are pressured to perform, not necessarily pressured to learn deeply and conceptually." Alarmingly, a young boy, who appeared to be about ten years old, reported, "You have to do well *now* so you can get in to a good college." According to the film's online advertisement, *Race to Nowhere* depicts "heartbreaking stories of students ... who have been pushed to the brink by over-scheduling, over-testing and the relentless pressure to achieve."[133]

The sentiments in *Race to Nowhere* are not new. In his book *Under Pressure*, journalist Carl Honoré admits his own desire to "harness [his son's] happiness, to hone and polish his talent, and to turn his art into an achievement" as part of a larger goal of trying to "steer [his] child to the top." According to Honoré, "The pressure to make the most of our kids feels all-consuming. We want them to have the best of everything. We want them to be artists, academics and athletes, to glide through life without hardship, pain or failure."[134] While the motivation to push our children may, in fact, come from a protective desire for them to "glide through life without hardship, pain or failure," our children do not necessarily experience it that way. Honoré writes that in many schools, "academic achievement is squeezing the lifeblood out of children."[135]

With respect to independent and international schools, the cultural and societal pressures that surround them have a long and deep history. The oldest independent schools in America, such as Phillips Academy Andover (est. 1778)[136] and Phillips Exeter Academy (est. 1781),[137] were developed in the likeness of their English predecessors, Eton College (est. 1440)[138] and Harrow School (est. 1572).[139] For many generations, these schools have tried

---

[132] http://www.racetonowhere.com/about-film.

[133] Ibid.

[134] C. Honore. *Under Pressure: Rescuing Our Children from the Culture of Hyperparenting*, (New York, Harper Collins, 2008) 3.

[135] Ibid., 114.

[136] http://www.andover.edu/About/PAHistory/Pages/default.aspx.

[137] http://www.exeter.edu.

[138] http://www.etoncollege.com/OurHistory.aspx.

[139] http://www.harrowschool.org.uk/index.aspx.

to attract "the best and brightest" students with the intention of preparing them for highly prosperous careers. For example, Eton College has "educated 19 British Prime Ministers and generations of aristocracy, and has been referred to as the chief nurse of England's statesmen."[140] (*In England, the term **public school** is used to refer to a small group of independent schools that are both expensive and exclusive, similar to America's "private schools.") "Early in the 20th century, a historian of Eton wrote, 'No other school can claim to have sent forth such a cohort of distinguished figures to make their mark on the world.'"[141] The current website for Eton College touts that Eton has "educated boys for six centuries"[142] and has continued Henry VI's original vision of providing a distinctive education ... to any boy who is offered a scholarship."[143]

In a similar way, many US independent schools promote in their mission statements that their schools strive to engage and educate the most capable students in the nation and the world. These students may not realize it immediately, but their being touted as some of the brightest students in the nation and the world is, itself, a pressure they may readily but naively absorb, a pressure they're expected to live up to as they try to make the grade. Ultimately, these same students are expected to apply and be accepted to selective top-tier colleges and universities. From this perspective, cultural and societal pressure is exemplified in—and may be defined as—these young students' daily efforts to conform to these tough and deeply ingrained expectations, and to adhere to this narrow academic pathway as if obligated to do so.

Pressure to Live in a Monoculture

As mentioned in the introduction to this book, F. S. Michaels's book *Monoculture: How One Story Is Changing Everything* helps to clarify how significant economic pressures are impacting independent and international schools. Michaels also describes a socioeconomic monoculture as occurring when "some subject rises to the top of our awareness, grabs

---

[140] "Eton—the establishment's choice." BBC News, 2 September 1998.
[141] Ralph Nevill, *Floreat Etona: Anecdotes and Memories of Eton College* (London: Macmillan, 1911), 1.
[142] http://www.etoncollege.com/Introduction.aspx.
[143] http://www.etoncollege.com/Scholarships.aspx.

hold of our imagination and shapes our lives."[144] For our purposes, the term "monoculture" sheds important light on the lure and power of high-performance secondary schools. Essentially, students' efforts to conform to strict expectations and to adhere to such a linear academic pathway—and schools' participation in, and compliance with, these widespread conformity efforts—seem to reflect a monoculture. Michaels claims that these "dominant ideas" form a "governing pattern that a culture obeys," and that this pattern "takes over other [patterns] and shrinks diversity."[145] According to Michaels, "When you're inside a monoculture, you tend to accept its definition of reality. You unconsciously believe and act on certain things, and disbelieve and fail to act on other things. That's the power of the monoculture; it's able to direct us without our knowing too much about it."[146] Finally, as Michaels asserts, "Over time, the monoculture evolves into a nearly invisible foundation that structures and shapes our lives, giving us our sense of how the world works. It shapes our ideas about what's normal and what we can expect from life. It channels our lives in a certain direction, setting out strict boundaries that we unconsciously learn to live inside."[147]

In this way, the academic pressures that students readily but naively absorb, that they're expected to live up to, reflect a hyperschooling educational monoculture. Like Michaels's socioeconomic monoculture, the hyperschooling monoculture "takes over" other ways of thinking and being. Over time, it acts as an "invisible foundation that structures and shapes [students'] lives, giving [them] a sense of how the world works." Essentially, it is from within this monoculture that students "accept its definition of reality" and strive to conform to its expectations for "across the board greatness" for the ultimate goal of applying to and attending a top-tier college or university.

Pressures Associated with Diversity

Students of various minority groups—be it race, ethnicity, religious affiliation, sexual orientation, gender identity, socioeconomic status/social class, health status, etc.—often experience considerable and unnecessary

---

[144] Michaels, *Monoculture*, 1.
[145] Ibid.
[146] Ibid.
[147] Ibid., 2.

pressure. Of note, Judith Ohikuare, in her 2013 *Atlantic* article "When Minority Students Attend Elite Private Schools," wrote "For years, [elite private schools were] largely inaccessible to minority and lower-income students. Maintaining [their] reputation as top-tier places of learning did not require administrators to extend invitations to those groups."[148] Further, Ohikuare quoted Myra McGovern of the National Association of Independent Schools as having said, "'In the 1960s and '70s there was a greater push to just integrate and assimilate; It wasn't until the late '70s and '80s that diversity became less about numbers, and more about having a community that was inclusive and drew strength from the diversity of the student body.'"[149] According to McGovern, "more independent schools are becoming invested in how diverse environments should *feel*, rather than only concentrating on what they should look like."[150] In her article, Ohikuare focused on the issues associated with being a racial minority student in elite secondary schools and stated that although "many parents of color send their children to exclusive, predominantly white schools in an attempt to give their kids a 'ticket to upward mobility,' these well-resourced institutions can fall short at nurturing minority students emotionally and intellectually."[151] Ohikuare reviewed the then-released documentary *American Promise*, which chronicled the experiences of two students of color who attended Dalton School in New York from kindergarten through their senior year of high school. According to Ohikuare, "The film reveals a hard truth about being a student of color at an elite school: Simply being admitted doesn't guarantee a smooth or successful educational journey."[152] The film conveys that when these two young boys began at Dalton, their parents were "filled with hope about their sons' new school."[153] Ohikuare noted further, however, "As the film progresses, [these parents] become less certain of Dalton's ability to improve their sons' lives. They realize that … Dalton's 'ticket to upward mobility' often came at a cost to their kids' success and self-esteem. 'We understood that this was

[148] http://www.theatlantic.com/education/archive/2013/12/when-minority-students-attend-elite-private-schools/282416/.
[149] http://www.theatlantic.com/education/archive/2013/12/when-minority-students-attend-elite-private-schools/282416/.
[150] Ibid.
[151] Ibid.
[152] Ibid.
[153] Ibid.

a school that the 1 percent sent their children to,' [one mother said], 'but not having grown up in that environment, neither of us understood the extent to which the social and emotional sides of our child's development would be at stake."[154] What are the implications, then, for students who spend much of their adolescence in this culturally skewed environment? How does being in the cultural minority differ from being in the cultural majority? What are the costs to those in the minority?

Many of the educators I interviewed expressed their dismay at the lack of true cultural diversity in their schools. One such educator stated, "We seem to think that by bringing culturally diverse students here, that we've covered it ... but we haven't. Once these students from different cultures, different countries and even different continents arrive here, we don't do enough to make them feel truly included. As a result, many of these students feel culturally dislocated."[155] For these students—for *any* students who perceive themselves to be one of a minority reflecting *any* of the classifications listed above—feeling "culturally dislocated" represents another layer of pressure.

Lorene Cary's 1991 autobiography, *Black Ice*, chronicled her own pressured adolescent years spent as a boarding student in the early 1970s at one of America's most prominent independent schools. Cary recounted how, as an African American student, she had initially felt so out of place there and had wondered to herself, "Were we black kids a social experiment? Were we imported to help round out the white kids' education?"[156] Cary reported further that she "knew [she] would emerge from [that school] changed, but [she] didn't know how, and [she] did not trust [her] white teachers and guardians to guide [her.] What would this education do to [her?] What was [she] to do with it?"[157] While Cary clearly knew that "this education [would be] more than knowledge, [and] could mean credentials, self-confidence [and] power," [158] she was not able to anticipate the degree to which that school "had shaken [her], or how damaged and fraudulent and traitorous"[159] she would feel when she graduated. Interestingly, as a young adult, Cary returned to teach at that same school and, later, to serve as

---

[154] Ibid.

[155] Anonymous.

[156] L. Cary, *Black Ice* (New York, Vintage Books, 1991), 5.

[157] Ibid.

[158] Ibid., 8.

[159] Ibid., 4.

one of its trustees. In *Black Ice*, Cary not only recalled her own pressured adolescent experiences, but she also recalled having eventually coached her African American students, "Try to think of [the school] as your school, too, not as a white place where [you're] trespassing."[160]

Trespassing? Even though they had been "accepted," did these students of color feel then—do they feel now—like they were/are attending someone else's school without real permission?

For another example, consider Deandre, an African American boy from St. Louis, whose pressures manifest as an entirely different issue. Deandre had learned about independent schools during his seventh grade science class, as his teacher, Mr. Rodriquez, had graduated from one in 1989. Deandre was a good overall student, but he had done particularly well in his math and science courses. Mr. Rodriquez had taken a genuine interest in Deandre and, eventually, took the risk of mentioning applying to some of the New England boarding schools to Deandre's mother, encouraging that she consider allowing Deandre to apply. Mr. Rodriquez explained that many of those schools not only offered generous financial aid to families who could not afford them, but also, that most of the schools were committed to attracting and enrolling academically talented students from diverse backgrounds, not just from the affluent white communities from which most students have come for many years.

In the late fall of his eighth-grade year, after months of careful reflection and deliberation with his mother, Deandre submitted applications to three independent boarding schools. In March, Deandre was overjoyed not only to have been accepted at his first-choice school, but also, to realize that his admission included a full scholarship, meaning that his mother would not be required to pay any tuition costs for the next four years. Suddenly, Deandre became very nervous, but, also, he began to realize the implications of his admission to such an impressive school. Going to *this* school could open all kinds of opportunities for Deandre! As a capable math and science student, Deandre had already dreamed of becoming a doctor and of opening an urban health clinic to provide quality medical services to so many families around his own neighborhood who had not had access to adequate health care. More immediately, however, having perused the school's viewbook that had been included in the application packet, Deandre had begun to imagine himself sitting at one of the school's

---

[160] Ibid., 5.

"Harkness tables,"[161] engaging in stimulating discussions with his teachers and fellow students, soaking up the lessons of the day. Deandre began to see himself there ... and he liked it.

While he had expected some aspects of this transition to be challenging, Deandre recalled his arrival and initial few months as "the biggest culture shock of my life." "It was so tough for me to leave home, to leave my brother, sister, and my mom behind, and to really leave the ghetto ... the hood. Even though I was made fun of in grade school (for being smart), and was bullied for not giving test answers to my friends, even though I was kinda relieved to leave that, and come to a school where everyone was smart, where everyone took school as seriously as I did, I still had to leave my family behind, and when you do that, things fall apart!"

Deandre characterized the personal costs of coming away to boarding school as "the great divide," and reflected on the contradictory feelings he still experiences today, several years after having graduated. "For thirteen years, you come to love all these great things with your family, and then, all of a sudden, you're gone ... for four years! Ironically, once I was there, I hated going home ... absolutely hated it. I used to try to stay at school as long as I could. During summers, I never went home. I used to find some way to work or go to a summer-study program so I could avoid going back to St. Louis. It was hard because I put so much energy into trying to fit in at my new school, into learning and adapting in that world. So, whenever I'd go home, where no one knows about these schools, where no one understands them, and mostly, where no one even cares about them, it was like impossible to be accepted again by my own family. I mean ... I came home after graduating and some of my own family members didn't even recognize me. Imagine going back to your own neighborhood and having people say, 'Who are you?' I remember learning about The Great Divide in our history class and thinking to myself, 'that's like my whole life now ... one big great divide,' and it's something I work on still ... years after graduating from high school. It's a constant struggle."

For a different—but no less burdening—example of these minority-related pressures, meet Toni, a sophomore girl whose physical appearance and socioeconomic status easily classified her as one of the white majority. Toni had scheduled an appointment to talk about her increasing sleep

[161] J. S. Cadwell and J. Quinn, (eds.), "A Classroom Revolution: Reflections on Harkness Learning and Teaching," Phillips Exeter Academy, 2015.

difficulty that was interfering with key aspects of her everyday function-ing: paying attention in classes; getting homework done; socializing with friends, and, in general, managing increasing feelings of anxiety. About a month earlier, Toni had told her parents about her romantic feelings for another girl at school—feelings Toni had experienced many times before regarding other girls but had never acknowledged to her parents—and that conversation with her parents had not gone well. As Toni reported, "My father seemed pretty neutral about it, maybe even accepting, but my mother tried to tell me, 'this is just a phase ... you're not a lesbian,' and just seemed to reject my feelings completely ... it felt like she was rejecting me." For the next two years, Toni and I met regularly as we gradually un-packed and discussed many facets of her life, particularly those relevant to Toni's emerging identity as a homosexual young woman. Most of Toni's early anxiety seemed associated with her having felt "rejected" by her own mother, a status that eventually changed as her parents engaged their own process of trying understand their daughter. Sadly, however, Toni also ac-knowledged underlying feelings of fear of losing some friends, as she had already experienced isolation and rebuff from some of these "friends" in the heterosexual majority. At times, Toni endured name-calling and other insults, encounters that left her feeling hurt, scared, and confused, feelings that only reinforced her initial anxieties about wanting to be accepted for who she truly was—and interestingly, feelings she had actually experi-enced earlier when she was one of the *presumed* majority, before she came out. Not surprisingly, many LGBT teens report higher incidences of both anxiety and depression, and it is now well-known that LGBT adolescents manifest a higher rate of suicide attempts. According to Brian Mustanski, PhD, associate professor at Northwestern University, who conducted lon-gitudinal research with a group of LGBT youth to learn about their suicide attempts, "the rate of lifetime suicide attempts [for LGBT teens] is over 30% which is much higher than in the general population of 16-20 year olds."[162]

Toni's experience of finding herself in a homosexual minority, and from that stance, struggling to fit in with those in the heterosexual major-ity, is another example of feeling "culturally dislocated." The same could be

---

[162] B. Mustanski and R. Liu, "A Longitudinal Study of Predictors of Suicide Attempts Among Lesbian, Gay, Bisexual, and Transgender Youth," *Archives of Sexual Behavior* 42, no. 3 (2013): 437–48.

said for *any* student who finds herself or himself in other so-called minority groups who "often experience considerable and unnecessary pressure."

Finally, another experience of feeling "culturally dislocated" that is common in US independent schools—but is particularly relevant in most international schools—pertains to students commonly termed "TCKs," or "third culture kids." These are students who grow up in countries and cultures that are different than their home/passport cultures; students who move frequently from country to country because of their parents' careers (in business, government, education, military, or missionary jobs), and although these students learn to appreciate a variety of diverse cultures and civilizations, they rarely feel at home in any of them. For example, Leah came to a US boarding school to begin the ninth grade. Leah is a passport-carrying American citizen who was born in Thailand and grew up attending international schools and/or American schools in that "host culture."[163] Leah's "first culture"[164] is that of her American-born parents—American. Leah's "second culture"[165] is that of her upbringing or "host culture"—Thailand. Leah's "third culture"[166] is defined as "a culture between cultures, an interstitial culture, and as the shared lifestyle of the expatriate community."[167] When Leah arrived in the United States for boarding school, although she *felt* extremely "culturally dislocated," she did not *look like* the other students who were also feeling that way. Essentially, because of her Caucasian American appearance and advanced English language abilities, Leah was frequently overlooked as a culturally dislocated kid, and did not get the support she desperately needed.

Within international schools, because "TCKs move back and forth from one culture to another *before* they have completed the critical task of forming a sense of their own personal or cultural identity,"[168] they often struggle more than even they might acknowledge to either themselves or to others around them. Since "understanding who we are and where we belong is a developmental task that takes place in the context of the

---

[163] D. C. Pollock and R. E. Van Reken, *Third Culture Kids: Growing Up among Worlds*, rev. ed., 2009 (Boston, Nicholas Brealey, 2001), 14.
[164] Ibid.
[165] Ibid.
[166] Ibid.
[167] Ibid.
[168] Ibid., 40.

surrounding community,"[169] the frequency of their moving from culture to culture—their characteristically nomadic lifestyle—predictably interferes with this important developmental task. Consequently, many TCKs report "feelings of rootlessness, restlessness, alienation, a confusion of identity, and a lack of true cultural balance."[170] While these students have also been described as "internationally minded, tolerant and respectful of diversity, culturally accepting, lacking in prejudice, 'colorblind,' less disposed to stereotyping, etc.,"[171] **at what cost** do they acquire these attributes? "According to Norma McCaig, who coined the moniker "global nomads" [to further describe TCKs], there's this myth of resiliency: the sense of loss is pretty profound. Sometimes these children have real problems feeling connected."[172]

As detailed throughout in this section, the pressures associated with being in *any* minority group are not "minor" and often reflect just one of the combined pressures adolescents confront in high performance secondary schools around the world. As stated beautifully by David Pollock and Ruth Van Reken, "All this talk about the third culture [or about any other students of a minority group] should not distract us from understanding the most critical part of the TCK [or the minority student] definition, the fact that a TCK [or any minority student] **is a person**."[173] Further, Pollock and Van Reken declare, "Sometimes TCKs [and minority students] spend so much time feeling different from people in the dominant culture around them that they (or those who notice these differences) begin to feel TCKs [or minority students] are, in fact, intrinsically different—some sort of special breed of being. While their experiences may be different from other people's, TCKs [and all minority students] were created with the same need that non-TCKs [and non-minority students] have for building relationships in which they love and are loved, ones in which they know others and are known by them. They need a sense of purpose and meaning in their lives and have the same capacities to think, learn, create, and make choices as others do."[174]

---

[169] Ibid., 43.

[170] E. Zilber, *Third Culture Kids: The Children of Educators in International Schools* (Woodbridge, UK. John Catt Educational, 2009), location 1221 of 4987, Kindle ed.

[171] Ibid., location 1176 of 4987, Kindle ed.

[172] Ibid., location 1222 of 4987, Kindle ed.

[173] Pollock and Van Reken, *Third Culture Kids*, 20.

[174] Ibid.

To conclude this section, if Myra McGovern of NAIS were to speak again today, I can imagine her saying, "More independent and international schools are becoming invested in how diverse environments should *feel*, rather than only concentrating on what they should look like."[175] Further, in light of all the pressures we have just reviewed that are associated with diversity, as the educator mentioned earlier stated, it seems true that "We don't do enough to make [minority students and TCKs] feel truly included. As a result, many of these students feel culturally dislocated."[176]

Pressure of Taking on Too Much Too Soon

Another source of pressure derives from the common belief that one must earn top grades *now* in order to have the best opportunities *later*. While many parents and students maintain a balanced perspective on this basic tenet, some take it to an extreme where it can lead to maladaptive perfectionism characterized by "flawlessness and setting excessively high performance standards, accompanied by overly critical self-evaluations and concerns regarding others' evaluations."[177] As one educator commented, "So many of my students have no time for the present; they're always thinking of, and preparing for, three to four years from now … for college." Another protested that "students face so many societal pressures to be more mature, and to be more sophisticated socially, sexually and academically before they're ready … that they seem to feel a responsibility for things that are more typical of adults." Further, many students feel pressured to prepare a career path before they've even applied to college! Describing the weight of this pressure, one parent lamented that her son "seems too serious, too early."

"From an early age, we're told that education is the key to one's success in life. Study hard! Get good grades! Go to college! And by making education freely available to all children, we're giving everyone an equal opportunity to succeed in life,"[178] says Kim Jones, CEO of Curriki, an online international community of learners. Further, according to Public Broadcasting Service, over time, the following have all been goals of education:

---

[175] http://www.theatlantic.com/education/archive/2013/12/when-minority-students-attend-elite-private-schools/282416/.

[176] Anonymous.

[177] http://en.wikipedia.org/wiki/Perfectionism_(psychology).

[178] http://www.forbes.com/sites/sap/2012/08/15/what-is-the-purpose-of-education/.

- To prepare children for citizenship
- To cultivate a skilled workforce
- To teach cultural literacy
- To prepare students for college
- To help students become critical thinkers
- To help students compete in a global marketplace[179]

A dictionary definition of the word *educate* refers to "developing the faculties and powers of a person by teaching."[180] Education has always entailed a process of deliberate, intentional skill-building and knowledge gathering, and of accruing these skills and lessons for later use. Even Socrates, the ancient Greek philosopher widely credited for laying the foundation for Western philosophy,[181] is reported by Plato to have said, "The unexamined life is not worth living."[182] To be sure, historical and contemporary societies have invested greatly in the basic belief that education is an important, if not necessary, part of living a meaningful and productive life.

While education may be one of the "keys to success in life," for some students—as we've already reviewed in a discussion about hyperschooling—too much education, too soon, can be damaging. There is something wrong with a ten-year-old boy reporting in *Race to Nowhere* that "You have to do well now so you can get in to a good college." Notably, in addition to his thinking about "the unexamined life not being worth living," Socrates also asked the Athenians, "Are you not ashamed of your eagerness to possess as much wealth, reputation, and honors as possible, while you do not care for nor give thought to wisdom and truth, or the best possible state of your soul?"[183] Socrates later stated, "For I go around doing nothing but persuading both young and old among you not to care for your body or your wealth in preference to or as strongly as for the best possible state of your soul."[184] After many years of working in high-achieving secondary schools, providing psychotherapy to teenagers who experience chronic anxiety and depression, many of whom struggle with self-destructive behavior, I can say with conviction that *theirs* are the symptoms of unhealthy souls.

[179] http://www.pbs.org/kcet/publicschool/get_involved/guide_p2.html.
[180] http://dictionary.reference.com/browse/educate.
[181] http://en.wikiquote.org/wiki/Socrates.
[182] http://www.guardian.co.uk/theguardian/2005/may/12/features11.g24.
[183] http://www.mesacc.edu/~davpy35701/text/plato-apology.html, #14.
[184] Ibid.

About two thousand five hundred years after Socrates lived, Dr. Thomas Moore, in his book *Care of the Soul* wrote, "The great malady of the twentieth century, implicated in all our troubles and affecting us individually and socially, is loss of soul. When soul is neglected, it doesn't just go away; it appears symptomatically in obsessions, addictions, violence and loss of meaning. Our temptation is to isolate these symptoms or to try to eradicate them one by one; but the root problem is that we have lost our wisdom about the soul, even our interest in it."[185] In an online audio interview, Dr. Moore claimed, "The soul of a person is what makes that person who he or she is."[186] Within this framework, symptoms such as anxiety and depression may be seen as physical and/or psychological signs that communicate that *at this time*, the person is functioning in ways that are incongruent with who he or she is. For teenagers, because they exist in such a developmentally sensitive period, timing is critical. Therefore, this experience may be even more disconcerting as, for them, the very concept of "who he or she is" is, itself, still developing. From this perspective, *Race to Nowhere*'s "heartbreaking stories of students who have been pushed to the brink by over-scheduling, over-testing and by the relentless pressure to achieve" suggest little about these students' "success in life," and instead, much about their feeling mistreated.

Perhaps the most extreme examples of unhealthy student souls may be found in Korean and Chinese "cram schools." In a 2011 *Time Magazine* article entitled "Teacher, Leave Those Kids Alone," Amanda Ripley wrote about South Korea's government-sanctioned crackdown on cram schools, also known as "hagwons," educational establishments attended by many Korean children *after* they have completed their full school day.[187] Ripley explained that "cramming is deeply embedded in Asia, where top grades—and often nothing else—have long been prized as essential for professional success,"[188] and that "South Korean kids gorge themselves on studying for one reason: to get into one of the country's top universities. The slots are too few—and the reward for getting in too great. 'Where you attend university haunts you for the rest of your life,' says Lee Beom, a former cram-school instructor who now works on reform in the Seoul metropolitan office of

---

[185] Thomas Moore, *Care of the Soul* (New York, HarperCollins, 1992), xi.
[186] http://www.youtube.com/watch?v=yzPdtY-qybQ.
[187] A. Ripley, in Time, September 25, 2011.
[188] Ibid.

education."[189] Appropriately, Ripley referred to this government-sanctioned crackdown on hagwons as "one part of South Korea's larger quest to tame the country's culture of educational masochism."[190] Tellingly, in his most recent book, Dr. Ken Robinson highlights that South Korea "has ranked in the top five of every PISA* program [and] spends about $8,200 on each student, [an amount that] represents almost 8 percent of the country's GDP, the second highest among OECD countries.[191] Further, "South Korea parents spend thousands of dollars on after-school tuition, but the real cost of South Korea's high performance on international tests is very much higher: the country now has the highest suicide rate of all industrialized OECD countries."[192]

*Program for International Student Assessment, a worldwide study by the Organization for Economic Co-operation and Development (OECD) in member and nonmember nations of fifteen-year-old students' scholastic performance in mathematics, science, and reading. [193]

Pressure to Demonstrate Executive Functioning Mastery

The relationship between emerging executive functions and the development of the prefrontal cortex is rather compelling. Over the past decade, educators and parents alike have been flooded with information about students needing a repertoire of executive functions in order to succeed in school. Interestingly, the very basis for the concept of executive functions first arose in the late 1840s when a New Hampshire small-town physician, Dr. John Martyn Harlow, was suddenly faced with a young adult patient who had suffered a traumatic brain injury. In late September of 1848, Phineas Gage, a railroad blasting crew foreman, was impaled through the

---

[189] Ibid.

[190] Ibid.

[191] "South Korea: System and School Organization," NCEE, www.ncee.org/programs-affiliates/center-on-international-education-benchmarking/top-performing-countries/south-korea-overview/south-korea-system-and-school-organization/. (Retrieved from R. Robinson and L. Aronica, *Creative Schools: The Grassroots Revolution That's Transforming Education* (Viking, 2015), 23.

[192] Reeta Chakrabarti, "South Korea Schools: Long Days, High Results," BBC.com, December 2, 2013. www.bbc.com/news/education-25187993. (Retrieved from: K. Robinson and L. Aronica, *Creative Schools: The Grassroots Revolution That's Transforming Education* (New York, Viking, 2015), 23.

[193] Kathleen Berger, *Invitation to the Life Span*, 2nd ed. (New York, Worth. 2013)

head by a crowbar-like iron rod after a sudden explosion at the worksite. Reportedly, this explosion propelled the iron rod "like a rocket" as it "entered the [left] side of [Mr. Gage's] face ... passing back of the left eye, and out at the top of the head."[194] Surprisingly, Gage survived this shocking event. Further, it was because of that unexpected reality that Dr. Harlow endeavored to understand the functions associated with the frontal lobe,[195] the region of Gage's brain most impacted by the accident, as Gage suddenly showed dramatic, negative changes in his personality. Prior to the accident, Phineas Gage had been considered by his employer as "an efficient and capable foreman ... a shrewd, smart businessman, very energetic and persistent in *executing* (emphasis added) all his plans of operation."[196] However, in the months and years after the accident, Gage was describe as "fitful, irreverent, indulging at times in the grossest profanity (which was not previously his custom), manifesting but little deference for his fellows, impatient of restraint or advice when it conflicts with his desires, at times pertinaciously obstinate, yet capricious and vacillating, devising many plans of future operations, which are no sooner arranged than they are abandoned in turn for others appearing more feasible."[197] It was this list of Phineas Gage's immediate and dramatic personality changes that led to years of subsequent inquiry into what we now call these self-regulating capacities, the executive functions.

Over time, executive functions "have been referred to in the popular press as the CEO of the brain."[198] Further, these basic regulatory functions have also been "accompanied by an anatomical reference of the location of this 'chief executive' as being housed in the frontal lobes."[199] While Phineas Gage's injuries in 1848 certainly pointed to the prefrontal cortex (PFC) in a causative way, modern brain imaging techniques have revealed that the brain is so much more networked than earlier scientists once believed. As present-day neurologists and neuropsychologists have been able to show,

---

[194] http://en.wikipedia.org/wiki/Phineas_Gage.

[195] J. M. Harlow, "Passage of an iron rod through the head," *Boston Medical and Surgical Journal* 39 (1848): 389–93. (Retrieved from: R. A. Barkley, (2012). *Executive Functions: What They Are, How They Work, and Why They Evolved* (New York, Guildford Press, Location 148 or 5476, Kindle edition).

[196] http://en.wikipedia.org/wiki/Phineas_Gage.

[197] Ibid.

[198] G. McCloskey, L. A. Perkins, and R. Van Divner, *Assessment and Intervention for Executive Function Difficulties* (New York: Routledge Taylor & Francis Group, 2009), 13.

[199] Ibid.

"executive functions [are] not exclusively a function of the PFC given that the PFC has various networks of connections to other cortical and sub-cortical regions as well as to the basal ganglia, amygdala and limbic system, and cerebellum."[200] At the present time, "executive functions can be thought of as a set of multiple cognitive capacities that act in a coordinated way ... as directive capacities that are responsible for a person's ability to engage in purposeful, organized, strategic, self-regulated, goal directed processing of perceptions, emotions, thoughts and actions. As a collection of directive capacities, executive functions *cue the use* (emphasis added) of other mental capacities such as reasoning, language and visuospatial representation."[201]

As mentioned earlier, most independent and international schools maintain rigorous admissions procedures by which talented and motivated students are invited to apply, knowing in advance that only a small percentage of these applicants will be admitted. Presumably, most of the admitted students have demonstrated their "reasoning, language and visuospatial" strengths to date. It is noteworthy, though, that most of these schools claim that successful applicants should be able to demonstrate intellectual curiosity and prior academic success, strong interpersonal skills and a readiness to study in a diverse environment, varied athletic abilities, an interest in music and/or in visual or performing arts, established study habits as well as organizational and time management skills, and, ideally, a demonstrated commitment to some kind of service in their local communities. Wow! That is a tall order. These applicants are early adolescents: they're thirteen to fifteen years old. While their "reasoning, language and visuospatial" skills may have gotten them this far, once admitted, they'll soon need to demonstrate their still-developing "directive capacities," too, those behind-the-scenes skills they'll need in order to engage their new school in a "purposeful, organized, strategic, self-regulated and goal-directed" manner that enables the "processing of their perceptions, emotions, thoughts and actions" within the rigors of their new school world. As McCloskey notes, these are the capacities that *cue the use* of the students' reasoning,

---

[200] M. B. Denckla, (1996). "A theory and model of executive function: a neuropsychological perspective," in G. R. Lyon and N. A. Krasnegor (eds.), *Attention, memory and executive function* (pp. 263-278), Baltimore: Brookes. (Retrieved from: R. A. Barkley, *Executive Functions: What They Are, How They Work, and Why They Evolved* (New York, Guildford Press. Location 157 of 5476, Kindle edition, 2012).

[201] McCloskey, Perkins, and Van Divner, *Assessment and Intervention*, 15.

language, and visuospatial abilities. The question is this: Will these newly admitted early-adolescents be able to activate, *on their own*, the appropriate set of directive capacities, their presumed "self-disciplined study habits, organizational abilities and time management skills," in order to adapt to their new schools' rigorous demands? Doubtful ... at least not without some discomfort or trouble in the process. No wonder so many of these intelligent, accomplished—and admitted—students often find themselves in academic, emotional, and/or behavioral disarray.

One way of breaking this down is to consider the very notion of intelligence. To be sure, all newly admitted students are considered to be intelligent, but what does that really mean?

In his 2005 edition of *Cognitive Psychology*, psychologist Robert Sternberg defines intelligence as "the capacity to learn from experience, using metacognitive processes to enhance learning, and the ability to adapt to the surrounding environment, which may require different adaptations within social and cultural contexts."[202] Further, McCloskey reminds us that the term "metacognitive processes" refers to "thinking about thinking," a term that is considered to be synonymous with executive functions.[203] Most important, as McCloskey also points out, is the very idea that true intelligence is less about acquired knowledge such as "What is the capital of Greece?" and more about an individual's "ability to adapt to the surrounding environment." It seems that *that* notion is most at stake here. Specifically, given that all our students are, presumably, developing within normal limits but at normally different rates, it is their struggle to adapt effectively, on our schools' imposed and compulsory schedules, that seems to present the most challenge. It is at these times that many students are trying out either new or not-yet-mastered executive capacities, skills to which they'll have much greater access as their brains gradually develop, with the right environmental stimulation, in their later adolescent years. This is a setup.

The process of executive function development is a slow, gradual process over time.[204] For example, McCloskey refers to inhibitory control as an executive skill that develops over many years. He states that "4-year-olds

[202] R. J. Sternberg, *Cognitive Psychology*, 4th ed. (Wadsworth Publishing. 2005), 485; in G. McCloskey, L. A. Perkins, and R. Van Divner, *Assessment and Intervention for Executive Function Difficulties*. (New York: Routledge Taylor & Francis Group, 2009) 21.

[203] McCloskey, Perkins, and Van Divner, *Assessment and Intervention*, 21.

[204] Ibid., 68.

are more proficient at cueing the Inhibit function than 2-year-olds," and "14-year-olds are more proficient than 4-year olds," while "24-year-olds are more proficient than 14-year-olds."[205] In this example, it's easy to appreciate that any individual's capacity to inhibit is, itself, a capacity that develops gradually, over a period of many years. McCloskey lists numerous capacities (organize, plan, initiate, monitor, shift, analyze, inhibit, switch, compare, sustain, retrieve, etc.), each of which may be considered an executive function, and each one, similar to our inhibitory control example, develops over a long period of time. In one of McCloskey's recent presentations when I was in his audience, Dr. McCloskey reported his typical response to parents and educators who frequently ask him about how long it takes to develop these skills: "Not forever, just longer than you'd like ... but you can bet on maturity."

To reinforce his point, McCloskey further claims that the wide variation in the development of executive capacities "is consistent with the wide variations in children's physical development."[206] In a convincing story, McCloskey asks his readers to consider the physical appearances of a typical group of young teenagers and to acknowledge that some of these young teens will "appear more similar to an elementary school-age child in both size and physical characteristics while others have the physical appearance of high school seniors."[207] McCloskey asserts, "This phenomenon of developmental variability is also present in terms of these students' abilities to use specific executive capacities."[208] Because the variation in executive function development is not as physically apparent among these students, many "barriers to this appreciation" exist and, therefore, set many students up for failure. McCloskey accurately declares that "students the same age but at varying stages of physical development are not expected to perform comparably in gym class (e.g., eighty-pound boys are not expected to wrestle 120-pound boys) in order to earn a passing grade, but all students are expected to perform comparably in terms of executive function-dependent capacities labeled as responsibility, self-organization, self-direction, self-discipline, and the like, in order to earn passing grades in most academic classes."[209]

---

[205] Ibid.
[206] Ibid., 70.
[207] Ibid., 70.
[208] Ibid.
[209] Ibid.

Finally, McCloskey accentuates that while all parents and educators naturally understand that students' physical development is out of their direct control, many of the same parents and educators seem to assume that students' brain development, especially in the form of executive function capacities, is well within their control, and that too frequently these young students' compromised executive performances get attributed either to their unwillingness and resistance, or to their presumed disabilities.[210] "Often in school settings, and even in many homes, there are very rigid expectations that executive function development be at a specific level for all same-aged children. The negative consequences applied to a child not performing up to the expected standards can be severe, unreasonable, and often uncompromising in nature. Appreciation of the natural variations in maturation of brain functions is crucial for ensuring appropriate educational experiences for those children who are demonstrating nothing more than natural delays in the development of executive function capacities."[211]

I am reminded of many students who have been referred to me for an assessment of their executive functioning abilities. Not surprisingly, on standard intelligence tests, these admitted-but-now-referred students typically score in the high average to superior range of cognitive ability, and exhibit greater—but not pathological—difficulties in some areas of executive functioning. For example, they lack effective organizational skills, they can't seem to manage their time efficiently, or they may struggle to balance competing academic and social demands. In some schools, these difficulties might not be so costly. However, in rigorous secondary schools, where being overscheduled and, for many, academically overloaded, is more the norm, these "natural delays in development" are frequently seen as deficiencies that, if left untreated, can be damaging. Specifically, in the face of many schools' complex and fast-paced curricula, many of these very intelligent students fall behind and, for the first time in their young lives, experience intense feelings of inadequacy and helplessness. Moreover, this normal variation in skill development often goes unnoticed as many adults unwittingly assume that students' executive functions just arrive "all at once" as a "package deal" or as a complete set. Consequently, when these otherwise bright and capable students do not evidence a knack for these important executive skills, they begin to feel pressured, marginalized, and at times pathologized.

---

[210] Ibid., 71.
[211] Ibid.

As one student recalled, "I was never a great student at my school, and that was really hard because I had thought of myself as a great student in middle school. I thought I was admitted because I *had been* a great student, but I guess that didn't turn out to be true. Anyway, after the first semester, my grades were really low so I had to meet with the learning specialist twice a week, get testing done to see if I had some kind of learning disability, and I had to go to study hall every school night from seven thirty to nine thirty ... and I hated that. I know it was meant to help me, but it really felt like punishment. Basically, I got put in all these like safety nets ... tutoring, learning specialist, study hall. Even though I never told to my friends how poorly I was doing, I think they knew because they didn't have to go to study hall ... and they knew that I did."

In light of what we now know about teenage brain development, about the slow and gradual maturing of executive functions, and about how environment has a considerable shaping influence on these processes, isn't it ironic that many of the most competitive secondary schools do not actually teach these skills to their students? For most incoming students, the transition from middle school to secondary school reflects a sudden "on-demand production circus."[212] According to Dr. McCloskey, for all students, "school is an imposition of executive function learning for which we should teach executive strategies, and students should be coached to practice them so they can become more self-regulating"[213] in their new environment. It would seem that if executive skills were so important for success within our highly rigorous environments, then at very least, we would provide some formal instruction in them.

In a recent TED Talk on "The Puzzle of Motivation,"[214] author and motivational speaker Daniel Pink claimed, "There is a mismatch between what science knows and what business does." In his talk, Mr. Pink refers to a particular research finding, one that was discovered over forty years ago and that now has four decades of evidence that reinforce it. After explaining this discovery in more detail, Mr. Pink claims that this has been "one of the most robust findings in social science, and also, one of the most ignored." In light of these words, then, it may not be an exaggeration to say: "There is a mismatch between what science *now* knows, and what *some*

---

[212] G. McCloskey, presentation on executive function delivered at NEALS Spring Conference, Forman School, Litchfield Connecticut, April 26, 2012.
[213] Ibid.
[214] http://video.success.com/from-the-magazine/daniel-pink-ted-talk-puzzle-motivation/.

schools do." Since neuroscience has confirmed that the prefrontal cortex is not fully developed until the mid-to-late twenties or even the early thirties, and since it has also confirmed that the prefrontal cortex is one of the primary regions responsible for learning and mastering essential "regulating and modulating" skills—a.k.a. "executive functions"—then why don't *all* schools—not just the rigorous and high-achieving schools—integrate the actual teaching and practicing of these very skills into their curricula? Might there be some negative implications of schools actually training their students in these essential skills?

We conclude this chapter having reviewed numerous and overlapping pressures that students experience as they try to "do it all," acquiescing to the mind-set that "only the best will do." As the title of this chapter suggests, many students are not dealing with just one or two pressures, such as the neurodevelopmental pressure to explore their own identity coupled with the pressure to achieve academically. On the contrary, in highly competitive schools, it is the rare student who is not dealing with multiple, ongoing, and intensifying pressures concurrently. It's not just the singular pressure to make the grade; or the specific pressure to cope with feeling culturally dislocated and trying to fit in; or the executive pressure to manage their time and organize their materials, space, and ideas effectively; or the obligatory pressure to "do well *now* so you can get in to a good college later."[215] For many students, it is *all of these pressures combined*, pressures that are fused with each other, that play off one another, and that too often build up and manifest in a variety of maladaptive and harmful ways.

---

[215] http://www.racetonowhere.com/about-film.

CHAPTER 5

The Heart of the Matter—
The Adolescent Brain

Having just reviewed the various combined pressures that all our students face, in one way or another, during their high school years, we are left with a fundamental question: Why does this matter so much now? I am reminded of a question I ask of most of my clients as we begin a psychotherapeutic relationship. While I am curious about why they have requested therapy, about the life conditions and/or relationship dynamics for which they are seeking support, I am equally curious—sometimes more curious—about why they have requested therapy *now*. Presumably, many of the circumstances for which they could have sought counseling before have existed for a while—sometimes for many years—so it is compelling to learn about what "tipped the scales," about what happened *recently* that motivated them to seek counseling help *now*.

This book is not about individual psychotherapeutic relationships, but the question of "why now?" is still quite pertinent. In the same way that the pressures that adolescents face in competitive academic environments could have been more carefully considered much earlier, something has happened *recently* that obliges us to more carefully consider them *now*. What didn't we know—even ten to fifteen years ago—that we know today that "calls us to action" and requires us to change now? Ironically, as the title of this chapter conveys, the answer to this fundamental question—the so-called "heart of the matter"—is in the adolescent brain. In this chapter, we review five compelling discoveries about adolescent development revealed by recent advances in neuroimaging, five discoveries that are critical and demanding of our appreciation and respect.

A note of caution is important here. While research has shown, un-equivocally, that the brain undergoes a second wave of development during the adolescent years[216]—and *that* is what our focus needs to be—it is also important to recognize that for *every* early adolescent, these profound hormonal, physical, sexual, cognitive, and emotional developments are in-terrelated and brilliantly coordinated within their own brain's vast network of neural connections and cortical regions. Further, this is what *every* early adolescent brings to her or his environment in a reciprocally interactive manner. While much is the same in these generalized adolescent devel-opments—they happen to all adolescents at the same time of their lives—much is also different, as each adolescent brings her or his own unique fam-ily, academic, and sociocultural history to bear on these changes. Finally, while these varied changes are, indeed, observable, none of them is separate or static. The living brain is always active and dynamic, and subject to environmental influence, and for these reasons, we must resist assuming that for any single adolescent, these changes are fixed and absolute, and, therefore, that they have direct implications for any individual's immediate life situation. However, this does *not* mean that we should disregard these critical changes, as they still reflect the "state of the art" of neuroscience in our era. From that vantage point, these changes provide us with some of the best insights currently available, and therefore, with a revised set of developmental guidelines for how we *now* need to understand the adoles-cents we teach every day. Having studied these changes for several years, I have come to understand the following five discoveries as essential to our mutual and collective understanding of our adolescent students.

1. Back to front development
2. The limbic system and the prefrontal cortex: uneven patterns of development
3. Neuroplasticity: neurons that fire together, wire together
4. Environment shapes the brain
5. Developmental sensitive (critical) periods

[216] S. J. Blakemore and U. Frith, *The Learning Brain: Lessons for Education* (Malden, MA.,Blackwell Publishing, 2005), 16.

Back to Front Development

Until recent advances in neuroimaging, most of our insights in this key area of development came from postmortem analyses. For example, "pioneering studies, mainly carried out by Peter Huttenlocher in Chicago in the 1970s and 1980s, demonstrated that the frontal cortex is the last brain region to develop in the human brain. [Huttenlocher] collected numerous postmortem brains from children, adolescents, and adults, and found that the frontal cortex was remarkably different in the brains of pre-pubescent children and post-pubescent adolescents."[217] Earlier studies from the late 1960s had already revealed that while the *volume* of the adolescent brain remained stable—it reaches its nearly adult size by early adolescence—there was an increase in *white matter* in the frontal cortex after puberty compared with before.[218] This increase in white matter meant there had been a buildup of myelin—the fatty tissue layer that facilitates neurotransmission—thereby increasing the transmission speed of neurons in the frontal cortex after puberty.[219] Subsequently, it was Huttenlocher who discovered the second big difference in the brains of prepubescent and postpubescent children. His postmortem studies revealed a significant *decrease* in the density of synapses in the frontal cortex after puberty, a finding that led to the realization that this decrease was likely the result of "synaptic pruning,"[220] the process by which "frequently used [synaptic] connections are strengthened and infrequently used [synaptic] connections are eliminated,"[221] or pruned away.

Subsequently, in the late 1990s, Dr. Jay Geidd of the National Institute of Mental Health, using time-lapsed photography of MRI scans of the brains of fifty-two developing children, each of whom was scanned four times over a fifteen-year period, produced a six-second video that showed the "ebb and flow of gray matter from ages five to twenty years."[222] These MRI scans not only reinforced but demonstrated, in real (time-lapsed) images of living human brains, what Peter Huttenlocher had observed many

---

[217] Ibid. 113.
[218] Ibid.
[219] Ibid.
[220] Ibid.
[221] Ibid. 22.
[222] http://www.nimh.nih.gov/news/science-news/2004/imaging-study-shows-brain-maturing.shtml.

years earlier in his postmortem studies. Geidd's research more definitively claimed that "the first areas to mature (e.g., extreme front and back of the brain) are those with the most basic functions, such as processing the senses and movement; and that areas involved in spatial orientation and language (parietal lobes) follow. Areas with more advanced functions—integrating information from the senses, reasoning, and other 'executive' functions (prefrontal cortex)—mature last."[223] Once again, isn't it ironic that the neurocognitive skills that develop *last* are the ones all new students need *first* to make a successful transition to high school, particularly to the most rigorous and high-achieving schools?

The Limbic System and the Prefrontal Cortex: Uneven Patterns of Development

The onset of puberty triggers a series of major changes in the limbic system, the brain's primary emotional processor that, as we have just discussed, develops long before the rational brain executive, the prefrontal cortex. Consequently, judgment, decision-making, and even reactions to everyday stressors can be overly affected by what can seem like the limbic system's unchecked and uninhibited emotions. Within the limbic system lies the amygdala, which is often considered the primary structure involved with sexual and emotional behavior.[224]

For our purposes, it is essential that we remind ourselves that because of these still-developing neural structures, "much of a teenager's response to the world is driven by emotion, not reason."[225] In fact, according to neurologist Francis Jensen, "Emotionally, the main difference between adults and adolescents is that there is much less activity in the frontal lobes of adolescents, making it harder for them to handle their emotions, especially in crisis situations."[226] Moreover, and critical to our present consideration of the pressures adolescents face in competitive academic environments, is the reality that "normal adolescents, even without any abnormal stress, have exaggerated amygdala functioning and therefore, increased stress

[223] Ibid.
[224] F. Jensen and A. E. Nutt, *The Teenage Brain: A Neuroscientist's Survival Guide to Raising Adolescents and Young Adults* (New York: Harper Collins, 2015), 46.
[225] Ibid., 171.
[226] Ibid.

reactions."[227] Accordingly, says Jensen, "So stress on top of an already over-active stress-response system can create havoc in the teen brain ... those who suffer [extreme anxiety] can become susceptible to crippling fear and anxiety throughout the remainder of their lives."[228]

Neuroplasticity: Neurons that Fire Together, Wire Together

Interestingly, another developmental principle of which we have known for over one hundred years—long before recent neuroscientists made the term more popular—is the concept of neuroplasticity, the basic reality that the brain is "plastic," or pliable and malleable. Reportedly, the term was first used in 1904 by psychologist Granville Stanley Hall, in his book, when he wrote that in adolescence, "character and personality are taking form, but everything is plastic."[229] Remarkably, even though the notion of plasticity had been discussed much earlier, many neuroscientists still maintained a scientific consensus throughout much of the twentieth century that brain structure was relatively immutable after a critical period of development during early childhood.[230] Fortunately, recent and unequivocal evidence gleaned from neuroimaging has replaced this earlier consensus. We now know for sure that neuroplasticity is a biochemical reality—that "neurons that fire together, wire together"—and that it is now well-known and defined as the brain's actual learning capacity, its "unique ability to mold itself,"[231] and as "the capacity for creating new neural connections and growing new neurons in response to experience."[232]

The concept of learning—"creating new neural connections and growing new neurons"—certainly implies *adding* new neural circuitry. However, an equally important feature of this learning process also involves *subtracting* unused circuitry, the process known as synaptic pruning. The

---

[227] Ibid., 176.

[228] Ibid., 176–77.

[229] G. S. Hall, *Adolescence: Its Psychology and Its Relations to Physiology, Anthropology, Sociology, Sex, Crime, Religion and Education* (New York: D. Appleton, 1904), in F. Jensen and A. E. Nutt, *The Teenage Brain: A Neuroscientist's Survival Guide to Raising Adolescents and Young Adults* (New York: Harper Collins, 2015), 18.

[230] P. Rakic, "Neurogenesis in adult primate neocortex: an evaluation of the evidence," *Nature Reviews Neuroscience* 3, no. 1 (January 2002): 65–71.

[231] Jensen and Nutt, *The Teenage Brain*, 68–69.

[232] D. Siegel, *Mindsight: The New Science of Personal Transformation* (New York, Bantam Books, 2010), 5.

following excerpt from an interview with Dr. Sarah-Jayne Blakemore of the Institute of Cognitive Neuroscience, University College London, helps to clarify this point.

> A very large pediatric neuroimaging project at the National Institute of Mental Health in Bethesda, Maryland, has [MRI] scanned thousands of children, adolescents and adults. They now have over 8,000 scans from two thousand individuals, and they put all this data together to form this semi-longitudinal dataset, which has shed a great deal of light on how the brain develops structurally during this period of life.
>
> One of the things they found is that the human cortex undergoes much more protracted development, both in terms of gray matter and white matter volumes, than was ever previously thought. We know, firstly, from this dataset, that in many different cortical regions, gray matter, which is mostly found in the cortex and contains cell bodies and synapses—the connections between cells—increases during childhood, peaks during mid to late childhood or early adolescence in most cortical areas, and then it declines really dramatically during adolescence [and] right into the 20s or even the 30s. We don't quite know what this corresponds to because MRI doesn't have the resolution to tell us about what's going on at a cellular level, or a synaptic level, but we know from postmortem human brain tissue studies that a large amount of synaptic pruning [occurs during these years]. In [these early years of] development, [these synapses] firstly increase in number and then decrease again, and that decrease in synapses is caused by synaptic pruning, where excess synapses are just eliminated. Synapses that aren't being used are pruned away or eliminated. That we know from postmortem human brain tissue studies. We think that the decrease in gray matter volume during the period of adolescence corresponds to synaptic pruning going on during the [same] period."[233]

---

[233] http://edge.org/conversation/sarah_jayne_blakemore-the-adolescent-brain.

What can we conclude from this? Extensive research has clearly shown that the brain is still developing during the period of adolescence: it is adaptable, and needs to be molded and shaped.[234] At the same time that the adolescent brain is capable of making and reinforcing new neural connections—also known as "learning"—it is simultaneously in the process of pruning other connections away, as it eliminates synapses that aren't being used. We have to ask ourselves, "What synapses are being strengthened and reinforced, and what synapses are being pruned away?" Critically, this process of strengthening certain synapses and eliminating certain others is, itself, the very process of shaping and molding the brain for present and future functioning, and it is *fully dependent on the environment* in which each "brain" exists. As we will review in the next section, the environment matters greatly and plays a fundamental and unavoidable role in the here-and-now development of each adolescent brain.

Environment Shapes the Brain

The discoveries we have already reviewed have intimated this notion that "environment shapes the brain." In the **Back to Front** section, we reviewed the increase of white matter in the frontal cortex after puberty, and the associated growth of myelin that increased the transmission speed of neurons at the same time. What we did not say in that section was that the only way to increase white matter, and, therefore, to grow myelin, is by way of experience, with regular and ongoing practice of various thinking, feeling, and behavior patterns within one's own environment.

Subsequently, in the **Neuroplasticity** section, we reviewed the reality that the brain is "plastic,"—or pliable and malleable—and that "neurons that fire together, wire together." What we did not say in that section was that neurons fire only in relation to experience, in relation to some stimulation either from within or from the outside environment. This principle not only reinforces the white matter and myelin discussion above, but in its most basic form, the principle of "neurons that fire together wire together" describes the basic learning process itself, which is subject to—and dependent on—the environment in which we live, work, and play. In this way, our very interactions with the immediate environment—our experiences, our relationships, our thoughts, our emotions, and our behaviors—play

---

[234] Blakemore and Frith, *The Learning Brain*, 121.

fundamental and inescapable roles in how we shape and mold our own brains. Daniel Siegel, author of *The Developing Mind: How Relationships and the Brain Interact to Shape Who We Are*, poignantly states, "We are always in a perpetual state of being created and creating ourselves."[235]

For an unsettling but very clear example of how environment shapes the brain, consider Romania's "lost generation" of an estimated "170,000 orphans [who] were discovered crammed into 700 institutions"[236] in 1989 during Nicolae Ceaușescu's dictatorship. Almost uniformly, these children were subject to overcrowded and unsanitary conditions in which their basic needs for hygiene, social interaction, and stimulation were neglected or ignored, sometimes for years. Not surprisingly, because of these chronically deprived conditions, these children manifested "profound developmental delays and abnormal social-emotional behavior."[237]

Finally, for another example, consider how overpressured environmental stimulation can lead not only to chronic anxiety, but also to elevated levels of cortisol, the stress hormone that is "believed to create a domino effect that hard-wires pathways between the hippocampus and the amygdala in a way that might create a vicious cycle by creating a brain that becomes predisposed to be in a constant state of fight-or-flight."[238] In this way, "chronic stress has the ability to flip a switch in stem cells that turns them into a type of cell that inhibits connections to the prefrontal cortex, which would improve learning and memory, but also, that lays down durable scaffolding linked to anxiety, depression and PTSD."[239] The short- and long-term effects of chronic stress—particularly for developing children and adolescents—must not be overlooked.

---

[235] D. J. Siegel, *The Developing Mind: How Relationships and the Brain Interact to Shape Who We Are* (Guilford Press, 1999), 221.
[236] K. Silver, *Romania's lost generation: inside the Iron Curtain's orphanages*, All in the Mind, Monday, 23 June 2014, 10:18AM (http://www.abc.net.au/radionational/programs/allinthemind/inside-the-iron-curtain's-orphanages/5543388).
[237] Ibid.
[238] C. Bergland, *Chronic Stress Can Damage Brain Structure and Connectivity*, (https://www.psychologytoday.com/blog/the-athletes-way/201402/chronic-stress-can-damage-brain-structure-and-connectivity) February 12, 2014.
[239] Ibid.

Developmental Sensitive (Critical) Periods

In the field of neuroscience, the term "sensitive periods"—historically called "critical periods"—refers to designated periods or developmental phases when individuals are maximally sensitive to environmental experiences in the process of shaping and molding the brain. Interestingly, for about forty years, there has been widespread agreement about an early childhood sensitive period, but only recent discoveries have confirmed that the brain is still developing throughout adolescence. Because of this history, the existence of an adolescent-phase sensitive period is relatively new. Developmental theorists and neuroscientists concur that the early childhood sensitive period begins at birth and extends until about the age of three years. Understandably, this is a time when appropriate environmental stimulation is crucial for normal brain development[240] because so much is changing within the infant-toddler-early childhood brain at such a dramatic rate. Similarly, recent findings in neuroscience suggest that the second sensitive period begins with the onset of puberty and extends for at least the next three years, as this is the only other time in the human lifespan when, once again, so much is changing at such a dramatic rate, and when appropriate environmental stimulation is crucial for normal brain development.[241] With this information, we now know that the period of adolescence—at least early adolescence—is a developmental sensitive period, "a window within which the effects of environmental stimulation on brain structure and function are maximized."[242]

The whole sensitive period hypothesis is based on "the one characteristic that the human brain shares with other species, that it exhibits marked changes with age, including [as we have just seen] the loss of neurons and the pruning of connections"[243] that occur at specific periods of development. Moreover, the entire field of human development—physical, cognitive, and emotional—is based on the fundamental principle that certain measurable changes occur in all human beings at predictable times throughout the lifespan, and that any individual's functional capacities are directly related to, and to a large extent determined by, her or his

---

[240] Blakemore and Frith, *The Learning Brain*, 112.
[241] Ibid.
[242] S. C. Thomas and C. P. Knowland, *European Psychiatric Review* 2009, "Touch Briefings," 2.
[243] Ibid.

position along that developmental continuum. Development, itself, refers to a series of stage-invariant phases through which we must pass in order to mature from infancy to old age. Obviously, it is physiologically impossible to progress from infancy to adulthood without first "growing up" through toddlerhood, childhood, and adolescence, in that order! In a related way, we don't expect infants to know how to read, nor do we expect eight-year-olds to reason like teenagers. However, when a child is *not* reading by the end of third grade, or when a teenager is *not* thinking abstractly by age sixteen, we get concerned. Why? Because, intuitively, we understand that human development holds sway, and that some demands are simply unfair to make if an individual is, developmentally, incapable of meeting them.

Before deliberating upon their current and future implications for our work, let's summarize these five neurodevelopmental certainties regarding adolescent brain development, certainties that *anyone* who works or lives with adolescents—educators and parents alike—*anywhere* in the world, needs to know and integrate into *everything* they do with teenagers.

1. The brain regions responsible for more advanced functions, such as integrating information from the senses, reasoning, and other "executive" functions (prefrontal cortex)—mature last.[244]

2. Because of their "exaggerated amygdala functioning" during this developmental phase, even adolescents *without* any abnormal stress possess overreactive stress-response systems.

3. Within the adolescent brain, "everything is plastic," and, therefore, dependent on the immediate environment for adding and strengthening new neural connections while simultaneously pruning or eliminating unused and, hopefully, unnecessary ones.

4. Adolescents' everyday experiences—their thoughts, feelings and behaviors—actually shape and mold their brains. As Daniel Siegel would say, adolescents are "being created and are creating themselves."

5. When thirteen- and fourteen year-old students arrive to our schools for the ninth and tenth grades, *all of them* have either just begun, or are just beginning, *the second most-developmentally sensitive period of their lives.* Just as when they were infants and

---

[244] http://www.nimh.nih.gov/news/science-news/2004/imaging-study-shows-brain-maturing.shtml.

toddlers, all early adolescents are, once again, "maximally sensitive to environmental experience in the process of shaping and molding their brains." Further, and of utmost importance, it is how *they* experience the school environment—not how we perceive them to be experiencing it—that matters most as it is *their* experiences that mold and shape *their* brains. In this way, *their* experiences in our schools have lifelong implications … for them.

Who knew that these five neurobiological realities have always been true about adolescent brain development? Understandably, until recent advances in neuroimaging, we have not had full access to these realities in the ways we do now. From this perspective, then, it is perfectly reasonable that, in the absence of these enlightening realities, we have not felt accountable to them; we have not expected ourselves to adhere to these realities as the developmental guidelines we now realize they are.

At the dawn of their adolescence, students enter these enriched and highly competitive schools and then experience an immediate uptick in what is expected of them. Not surprisingly, along with increased demands, these students also experience an increase in the stress they feel about trying to meet these new and complex demands. What happens when the demands they face outweigh their internal capacities and their external supports, and their stress soars out of balance? What happens when their stress gets extreme, when the pressures build too high or too quickly and students' initial "stress" turns to lasting anxiety? They shut down, but not necessarily all at once. Because many of these students lack the skill of expressing complicated feelings with words (many adults lack this ability, too!), they rarely just freeze or "stop dead in their tracks." Instead, they tend to exhibit a "slow burn" characterized by more frequent expressions of frustration, disillusionment, and, too often, shame. As we have already discussed, many of these students exhibit recognizable signs of increased stress, such as erratic academic performances and/or flat and sullen moods. Others develop intense feelings of anxiety and depression and then act out these feelings in a variety of disturbing ways. Given their biologically determined overreactive stress-response systems, many of these students simply can't tolerate the humiliation and shame associated with what *they* experience as repeated failures, so with their increasingly depressive mindsets, some contemplate suicide … and some of *these* students actually kill themselves.

I have not witnessed a sadder outcome of the unresolved conflict between developmental challenges and available supports than the one exposed by adolescent suicide. In the several cases with which I have been involved clinically, these still-developing and, therefore, highly vulnerable adolescents felt overwhelmed by the various burdens and pressures they faced. Tragically, they did not perceive that tangible and empathic supports were available. These teenagers reflect the claim that "depression emerges with such force and frequency in adolescence."[245] These were teenagers whose combined social, emotional, and/or academic challenges outweighed their developmental capacities to cope.

Importantly, these recurring cases of students with debilitating anxiety and depression, of students acting out feelings in either aggressive or self-injurious ways, and mostly of students contemplating and/or committing suicide, raise important questions for us—the adults who lead and teach in these schools—about the ways in which we conduct ourselves, and about our own willingness and/or readiness to modify our programs to meet our students—developmentally—where they are.

Neurodevelopmental Costs?

Before we can determine specific modifications in our schools, it may be helpful to consider a few questions that may help guide our thinking about trying to synchronize our curricular and extracurricular programs with these five neurodevelopmental realities.

1. In what ways are our overall curricular and extracurricular programs either consistent or inconsistent with the reality that "areas of the brain responsible for more advanced functions—particularly reasoning and executive functions—mature last?"
2. Given the fact that *all* early adolescents are subject to exaggerated amygdala functioning—such that their reactions to the world around them are driven more by emotion than by reason—and mostly, that "stress on top of an already over reactive stress-response system can create havoc in the teen brain," what might this tell us about our admitted practices of overscheduling, overworking, and/or overpressuring our students? Further, because of the obvious

[245] S. L. Andersen and M. H. Teicher, *Trends in Neurosciences* 31, no.4 (2008), 183.

differences between adolescents' still-developing emotional reactivity and adults' more-developed capacities in these areas, are we not liable to misjudge—to underestimate—the strength of *their* stress reactions?

3. Since we now know—unequivocally—that environment shapes the brain, how do the pressures that we impose impact our students, all of whom "are being created and are creating themselves" within these competitive and pressured environments?

4. Without a doubt, these five neurodevelopmental realities apply to *all* our students, not just the students we already observe to be struggling. In fact, the "ones we already see struggling" are likely to reflect the tip of the teen-stress iceberg. As some of the students I have mentioned in this book reflected, and as many others clearly show, many, many students in their pressured environments experience significant and ongoing stress, but they also possess rather sophisticated social skills—for better or worse—that conceal their stress, at least temporarily, and that fool many adults into thinking that the students are not that stressed at all. How can we begin to assess all our students in order to make these important determinations?

5. As we just mentioned, Andersen and Teicher's research on the neurobiological framework of adolescent depression clearly reveals "the surge of newly emergent cases" of depression in the early adolescent years, due largely to the uneven developmental patterns of the limbic system and the prefrontal cortex. In what ways might our overscheduling, overworking, and overpressuring our students contribute to students' emerging depressions?

Anxiety and Depression: The True Costs of Too Much Pressure

Take a closer look at the research on the neurobiological framework of adolescent depression conducted by Drs. Susan Andersen and Martin Teicher of McLean Hospital in Belmont, Massachusetts. In light of the developmental phenomena we have just reviewed, it is particularly striking that the "lifetime prevalence [of major depression] increases dramatically from one percent of the population under age twelve, to between seventeen and twenty five percent by the end of adolescence, [with] the greatest surge in newly emergent cases occurring between fifteen and eighteen years of age."[246] Why this sudden increase in the incidence of major depression? Are children just sinking into misery as their childhoods come to an end? Are they reacting to something toxic that we adults haven't considered or addressed? Perhaps, but in the same way that health professionals diagnose *un*healthy conditions (diseases, disorders, pathologies) by contrasting them to their knowledge of healthy functioning, given that we now know that "environment shapes the brain," this "surge of newly emergent cases" of depression tells us something critical about what these children are experiencing in *their* environments, something about their *un*healthy development there. For the "seventeen to twenty five percent" mentioned above, something in their environments is interfering with their previously healthy developmental trajectories, something we need to know lest we risk contributing to even more children's experience of major depression.

Not surprisingly, Andersen and Teicher write poignantly of "stress, sensitive periods and maturational events in adolescent brain development,"[247] and of their research that has contributed a compelling neurobiological perspective on adolescent depression. Further, they "provide an overview of how the maturation of specific brain regions and stress exposure during windows of vulnerability initiate a series of events that render adolescents exceptionally susceptible to the development of depression."[248]

Andersen and Teicher acknowledge that "this is a relatively new area of inquiry," and they recognize that while many studies have been done and that none of them can "provide evidence for a cause-and-effect relationship," many completed studies have still confirmed "morphological differences"—structural changes in specific brain areas, such as changes in volume/size—associated with exposure to early/chronic stress.[249] In their review of various studies, Andersen and Teicher found that early onset and longer duration of stressors were linked with greater morphological change.[250] While Andersen and Teicher admitted that this conclusion could be interpreted as an oversimplification, their overall findings still led to their proposing "that stress-susceptible brain regions have unique sensitive

---

[246] Ibid.
[247] Ibid.
[248] Ibid.
[249] Ibid., 186.
[250] Ibid., 187.

periods (or windows of vulnerability) to the effects of early stress."[251] In their conclusion, Andersen and Teicher stated: "Time is a crucial factor, both in terms of windows of vulnerability when brain regions might be maximally sensitive to environmental influences, and in the cascade of maturational events that lead to the unfolding of depression. The hippocampus and pre-frontal cortex can have early and late windows of vulnerability, and [they] serve respectively as targets for the predisposing and precipitating effects of stress. Alterations in the amygdala and nucleus accumbens might con-tribute, in turn, to the negative and positive affectivity symptoms seen in depression. Together, this model provides a neurobiological framework that potentially accounts for the emergence of depression during adolescence."[252]

While the specifics of neuroanatomy and the technical language in the paragraph above may seem, understandably, too complex for a lay-audience, readers are encouraged not to get bogged down there. Instead, the "big pic-ture" perspective is to direct our attention to the mere fact that Andersen and Teicher actually proposed—after having reviewed numerous studies of the inside of living human brains—that (1) "time is a crucial factor," (2) that there are "windows of vulnerability when [certain] brain regions may be maximally sensitive to environmental influences," and (3) that these brain regions "can have early and late windows of vulnerability" such that they may also "serve as targets for the predisposing and precipitating effects of stress."

Time is a crucial factor? Targets for the predisposing and precipitating effects of stress? Incredible. These discoveries, and these associated techni-cal and anatomically specific statements, simply did not exist in *any* studies about adolescent development as recently as ten to fifteen years ago! This changes everything.

As mentioned earlier, the relationship between human performance and feeling pressured was first documented in 1908 by psychologists Robert Yerkes and John Dodson, when they published what eventually became known as the Yerkes-Dodson law. This "law," also known as the "Inverted U Model," characterized "peak performance [as being] achieved when people experience a moderate level of pressure. When they experience too much or too little pressure, their performances decline, sometimes severely."[253]

---

[251] Ibid.
[252] Ibid., 189.
[253] http://www.mindtools.com/pages/article/inverted-u.htm.

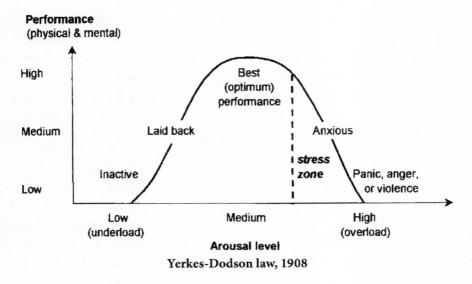

Yerkes-Dodson law, 1908

As the Yerkes-Dodson graph illustrates, performance is maximized at the top of the inverted U, where just enough pressure contributes to enhanced functioning. Further, the Yerkes-Dodson law also illustrates how performance diminishes rapidly as pressure intensifies. Of particular interest, Yerkes and Dodson describe the area beyond the peak-performance point as the "stress zone," the psychological space where anxiety remains constant, where individuals "fall apart under pressure," and where they become "overwhelmed by the volume and scale of competing demands on their attention, and may start to panic."[254]

While Yerkes' and Dodson's law has provided generalized information about the relationship between performance and stress for over a century, more recent studies relevant to adolescents' experience provide a more detailed analysis. Specifically, recent studies have identified that "anxiety disorders often precede the emergence of depression and identify children at risk for developing depression."[255] In their review, Andersen and Teicher

---

[254] http://www.mindtools.com/pages/article/inverted-u.htm.
[255] K. Beesdo *et al.*, "Incidence of social anxiety disorder and the consistent risk for secondary depression in the first three decades of life," *Arch. Gen. Psychiatry* 64 (2007): 903–12; D. E. Williamson et al. (2005), "A genetic epidemiological perspective on comorbidity of depression and anxiety," *Child Adolesc. Psychiatr. Clin. N. Am.* 14, 707–26.

cite a "triadic model" of adolescent depression,[256] one that highlights an inner, developmental dynamic between the regulatory and modulating functions of the prefrontal cortex and the emotion/affect-driving functions of the limbic system (amygdala and hippocampus). This model "postulates that adolescent depression emerges as limbic structures [that are] driving affect mature in advance of cortical structures [responsible for] providing regulatory control."[257]

For our purposes, this triadic model implies that for *all* adolescents, given their normally developing, overreactive stress-response systems, too much pressure can too easily result in neurobiological overload. Essentially, this is a state in which adolescents cannot effectively modulate their intensifying anxiety because the structure most responsible for regulating these emotions—the prefrontal cortex—is itself still developing. Most importantly, it is precisely because of this underdeveloped capacity to self-regulate and/or to modulate intense emotions that many adolescents act out their feelings in maladaptive ways when they feel overwhelmed. As I stated in the introduction, "*so many* teenagers in *so many* rigorous secondary schools everywhere are manifesting with *so many* of the same disturbing problems." Fundamentally, these teens are conveying that the many and combined pressures they encounter far exceed their developmental capacities to manage them.

Finally, these recent studies reinforce the notion that the entire adolescent era is a developmental sensitive period, and that environmental factors play a critical role in determining the overall quality of *any* adolescent's experience. Perhaps psychologist David Elkind, author of three editions of *The Hurried Child*, said it best: "In our information society, the brain has become the ultimate scientific authority."[258] Hopefully, we will take full advantage of the extraordinary richness of the scientific information now available as we consider new and more developmentally appropriate ways of educating and parenting our teenagers.

---

[256] M. Earnst *et al.*, "Triadic model of the neurobiology of motivated behavior in adolescence," *Psychol. Med.* 36 (2006): 299–12 (in S. L. Andersen and M. H. Teicher, *Trends in Neurosciences* 31, no. 4 (2008).

[257] Ibid.

[258] D. Elkind, *The Hurried Child: Growing Up Too Fast Too Soon*, 25th anniversary ed. (Boston, Da Capo Press, 2007), 108.

PART 3

We All Bear the Cost

CHAPTER 6

Fears that Paralyze

While many students do, indeed, thrive in these rigorous and high-achieving schools, many others struggle mightily in them, and some of *those* students exhibit very serious trouble. Do we really want to treat any of our students to an overscheduled, overworked, and sometimes, overwhelmed school experience only to risk *mis*treating and harming them? Do we really want to hyperschool our students and risk disturbing their otherwise healthy developmental trajectories? I don't think so, and from what hundreds of current educators and parents from competitive schools around the world have said, neither do they. Therefore, in an effort to both respect our students' development as well as honor our own stated commitments to "teaching our students in healthy and balanced ways" or to "having healthy children, above all else," I ask you, in the words of Leo Tolstoy, "What then must we do?"[259]

As we saw earlier in chapter 2, the *Immunity To Change*[260] paradigm enabled us to unearth and appropriately acknowledge the massive bind in which we live and work, a bind that, collectively, we co-construct and reinforce daily. Guided by this paradigm, we've been able to establish *that* we're in this bind, and that it occurs pervasively in competitive schools around the world. At this point, we need more information about *why* we're in this bind, and about *why* it seems so difficult to get out from under it. In this section, we explore our bind more deeply.

Recall that with remarkable consistency, all of the educators interviewed for this book named not only their binds, but also what Kegan and Lahey term as the interviewees' "competing commitments," those

---

[259] L. Tolstoy. *What Is to Be Done?* (Cambridge, England. Green Books. 1991)
[260] Kegan and Lahey, *Immunity to Change.*

commitments they have to *not* feeling the anxiety that accompanies the contradictory binds they're in. As Kegan and Lahey note, "The idea behind the immunity to change is that we do not merely have our fears; we sensibly, even artfully, protect ourselves from them. We create ways of dealing with the anxiety these fears provoke. We are not only afraid; we take action to combat our fears. We defend ourselves from what terrifies us. We are actively (but not necessarily consciously) committed to making sure the things we are afraid of do not happen."[261]

So at this point, we have to ask, "What is it, then, that is supposedly 'terrifying' us?" "What is this anxiety that our fears are provoking?" "From what fears are we 'sensibly, even artfully,' defending ourselves?" When asked about these issues directly, once again, these earnest educators candidly declared their "competing commitments," and in so doing, though unexpectedly, they also revealed their deeper underlying fears.

Recall the fears we've already reviewed, such as, "If we didn't over-schedule our students, or if we didn't assign them with too much homework, etc., we fear that we'd be seen as having lost our standards, and as lacking in rigor and excellence." Other educators admitted to a host of other underlying fears such as, "If we didn't … overschedule, assign too much work, etc., we fear that we'd be perceived as intellectually soft;" "then we might realize that we've become too wedded to the 'old ways' of maintaining our historic reputation;" "then we might find out that we've been wrong about these [unhealthy] practices all along, and that *that* would be humiliating." Finally, one administrator admitted, "If we actually gave in, and a developmentally reasonable schedule emerged, we might achieve a healthy balance for our students at the cost of our own distinctiveness; we fear that we might also lose our edge of excellence."

Referring back to the "**Mining the Fears**" section in chapter 2, the fears "of being perceived as intellectually soft;" "of not upholding our reputation;" of realizing "that we've been wrong about these [unhealthy] practices all along;" "of feeling depleted, overworked and unhealthy" and "of not having balanced lives of our own;" "of not being liked by our students;" "of having to face our own shortcomings;" "of having to make adjustments that could have an impact on our jobs;" and "of losing our distinctiveness," are all fears associated with underlying—and previously unacknowledged—commitments either to institutional protection ("to upholding our

261 Kegan and Lahey, *Immunity to Change*, 241.

reputation as a rigorous school") or to self-interest ("to not feeling depleted and overworked ..." and "to having balanced lives of our own"). By anyone's standards, and certainly by the standards of otherwise-esteemed educators, these are significant fears that, if they were to be realized, could trigger feelings of dread. For most educators, the anxiety associated with actually "being perceived as intellectually soft," or of actually realizing they've been "wrong" about these aspects of how they've been conducting business for many years, of actually "feeling depleted and overworked themselves" (more than they already do!), or of actually "having to face their own shortcomings" would be rather unsettling.

From this darker perspective, then, it makes perfect sense that these *would* be fears that we wouldn't "merely have," but rather, they'd be fears that we would "sensibly, even artfully," protect ourselves from feeling. Is it possible, then, that we have collectively and systematically "created ways of dealing with the anxiety these fears provoke?" Is our list of unhealthy practices—overscheduling our students, assigning them with too much work, expecting them to act as if they were adults, etc.—*also* a list of the practical ways we have "taken action to combat our fears?" From this perspective, it seems logical that we *would* "defend ourselves from what terrifies us," and that we *would* "be actively (but not necessarily consciously) committed to making sure" these unsettling fears never see the light of day.

Poignantly, we can now see that these unhealthy but widespread practices at competitive schools around the world seem to serve a very important function: to protect the schools and the adults who work there. Caught in an intense predicament between the parents, on the one hand, whose demand for these schools only increases, and the selective colleges, on the other hand, that rely on these schools for high-quality applicants, we have had to develop a complex set of self-protective practices to keep our schools in business. Moreover, and reinforcing the strength behind these competing commitments, *every* educator from the numerous independent, international and public schools I interviewed for this book recognized and acknowledged this systematic, self-protective effort. Without a doubt, this is a fundamental, if not critical, commitment. However, as fundamental and critical as it may be, it has one major flaw: it prevents educators from following through on their genuine commitments to "teach [their] students in healthy and balanced ways," and to "meet kids where they are."

As entrusted overseers of these schools, for us to do anything, deliberately, that contradicts who we are as educators, or that conflicts with who we are as well-intended human beings, understandably, leaves us feeling betrayed and disheartened. Operating in this perpetually compromised position, most of us "cope [as well as we can] within the world of our assumptive designs."[262] Sadly, we assume that this is our fate, so we proceed with business as usual. In my view, *this* is the real cost! Within the context of our own pressured environment, we live and work within the assumption that we're powerless in the face of this uncomfortable bind.

It is striking that under the veil of confidentiality and with my guarantee of complete anonymity, so many educators from competitive secondary schools in the United States, Europe, and Asia, felt safe enough to disclose their uncomfortable contradictory binds. Why did they do this? Why did so many educators risk speaking so openly about their raw vulnerabilities? I contend that not only are these educators authentically caring and dedicated individuals but, also, that they hope their collective voices can somehow ring as one loud and unified voice that calls out in support of changes that both respect their students' development, *and* that allow them—the adults—to resolve their own inner binds and experience even greater professional satisfaction and integrity.

How Did This Happen?

After all this lamenting about the adults, and about how collectively—but not quite consciously—committed they seem to be "to making sure their unsettling fears never see the light of day" within their schools, we have to ask, how did this happen? How did these talented educators, with vocation-like dedication, find themselves in such an awkward and disheartening bind?

In his recent book *Excellent Sheep: The Miseducation of the American Elite & the Way to a Meaningful Life*, William Deresiewicz chronicles, in great detail, the telling history of how, over a period of about 150 years, due to a succession of intertwined social, political, and economic forces, college admissions requirements—what Deresiewicz terms as "the fulcrum on which the system turns [as it] casts its shadow back over childhood and adolescence and forward over college and career, shaping the way that kids are raised and thus the people they become"[263]—colleges have transformed

---

[262] Kegan and Lahey, *How the Way We Talk*, 71.
[263] William Deresiewicz, *Excellent Sheep: The Miseductation of American Elite & the Way to a Meaningful Life* (New York: Free Press, 2014), 27.

from an "old aristocracy" model to the now-not-so-new "meritocracy" model,[264] or, as Deresiewicz poignantly describes it, "from caste, 'character,' and connections to scores and grades."[265]

Reportedly, during the years of the "aristocratic" model, while "admissions [to highly selective colleges] were based on entrance exams, kids from feeder schools would often be let in no matter how badly they did."[266] Deresiewicz reports that of the 405 Grotonians who applied to Harvard from 1906 to 1932, [Harvard] rejected three."[267] For Groton, that meant 402 admissions to Harvard over a twenty-six-year period, or an average of fifteen students per year ... at Harvard alone. Further, "as late as 1950, Harvard received only 13 applications for every 10 spots, while Yale's acceptance rate was 46 percent."[268]

As the new meritocratic system began to develop "on a monumental scale"[269] during the 1960s, the criteria for selective college admission, and therefore, the pressure on all high school students seeking admission to those colleges, became increasingly intensified. According to Deresiewicz, "the only thing that's changed since the mid-1960s is that everything has gotten inexorably worse: the admissions rates lower, the expectations higher, the competition fiercer, the pressure on students greater."[270]

Consider the following points of reference. "By 1968, the admissions rates at Harvard, Princeton and Yale had fallen to around 20%."[271] Today, the admissions rates at these same universities are around 6 percent, and as we have just seen in the 2016 admissions season, Stanford reported "an ultra-low admit rate of 4.7%."[272] Deresiewicz lists several other factors that, over the past forty to fifty years, have intensified the pressure. For example, in the 1970s, since the college-age cohort had increased, the number of students completing college degrees increased, too, making it "more imperative to distinguish yourself by going to a big-name school."[273] In addition,

---

[264] Ibid., 31.

[265] Ibid.

[266] Ibid., 29.

[267] Ibid.

[268] Ibid., 30.

[269] Ibid., 31.

[270] Ibid., 33.

[271] Ibid.

[272] www.washingtonpost.com/news/grade-point/wp/2016/04/05/stanford-dean-schools-ultra-low-admit-rate-not-something-to-boast-about/.

[273] Deresiewicz, *Excellent Sheep*, 33.

"colleges were letting it be known that they wanted as many Advanced Placement courses as possible on high school transcripts," thereby adding to the pressured menu of "requirements" to be met by younger adolescents. Further still, "over the last couple of decades, the admissions pool has gone from national to global."[274]

Recall, from chapter 1 the *New York Times* article from January 2013, "International Schools in China Point Students to the West," in which Lucy Hornby-Reuters reported, "The number of international schools registered in mainland China has soared in the past 12 years, to 338, from 22," and "Enrollment has risen 25 times in the same period, to 184,073 students." Also, recall the related *New York Times* piece, "International Schools Boom as More Seek Education in English" from April 2013, in which Joyce Lau reported, "As developed nations have become wealthier and as the world has become more multicultural, international schools have boomed. According to ISC Research in Britain, there are now 6,400 international schools all over the globe. In a decade, that number is expected to almost double."

All this information, from William Deresiewicz, from Lucy Hornby-Reuters, from Joyce Lau, from Ken Robinson and from a whole host of others, reinforces the reality that today's higher education environment is frequently characterized as one big educational arms race. Julie Lythcott-Haims, former Dean of Freshmen and Undergraduate Advising at Stanford University, defines this phenomenon as a "college admissions arms race"[275] and states, "There are a severely limited number of slots at the colleges we want our kids to attend, and an overabundance of people who want them. Hence the arms race."[276] Further, Gordon Winston of Williams College notes, "The essence of an arms race is *position*—how a country or university stands relative to others. No single institution alone can safely quit the race, even though all institutions, together, would be better off if everyone did."[277] This ongoing race for *position* translates to conditions of extreme and mutual competition. Sadly, as the competition escalates at the college level, younger adolescents who anticipate applying to these colleges are forced to pay an increasingly damaging price. At what cost?

---

[274] Deresiewicz, *Excellent Sheep*, 34.

[275] J. Lythcott-Haims, *How to Raise an Adult: Break Free of the Overparenting Trap and Prepare Your Kid for Success* (New York: Henry Holt, 2015), 56.

[276] Ibid.

[277] https://net.educause.edu/ir/library/pdf/ffp0103s.pdf (The Positional Arms Race In Higher Education).

Becoming Indistinguishable?

One of the most expensive developmental costs, it appears, is that most of these students are subject to imposed educational conformity. As Ken Robinson poignantly asserts, "The problem with conformity in education is that people are not standardized to begin with." Robinson defines educational conformity as "the institutional tendency to judge students by a single standard of ability and to treat those who don't meet it as 'less able' or 'disabled'—as deviations from the norm."[278] As I emphasized in the introduction to this book, "as more and more [required conformity] demands get piled on to [students'] already-frenetic schedules, [many of these students feel] overwhelmed, unheard, and at times, disillusioned." Too often, these are the students who are treated as "less able" or "disabled." Confused and frightened by their new negative status, many become anxious and depressed and then act out these feelings in a variety of harmful ways.

Interestingly, Ken Robinson's "problem with conformity" reflects the same phenomenon we reviewed in chapter 3 as Richard Perez-Pena alluded to the "deluge of applications" to the most selective colleges, and then reported that "most of the students [that these selective colleges] turned down are such strong candidates that many are indistinguishable from those who get in."[279] One of the major "costs" to developing adolescents is their being required, increasingly, to conform to the extent that they begin to act and look so much alike that they are seen as "indistinguishable"[280] from one another. As we also reviewed in chapter 4, renowned theorist Erik Erikson underscored the significance of the adolescent drive for identity as he wrote of teenagers' "persistent endeavor to define, over-define and redefine themselves and each other in often ruthless comparison"[281] to avoid a sense of role confusion, a condition Erikson described as "the horror of undefinedness."[282]

Hopefully, you recognize the uncanny similarity between the terms "indistinguishable" and "undefinedness." The first is defined as "unable to be recognized as different: impossible to distinguish clearly from something

---

[278] Robinson and Aronica, *Creative Schools*, 36.

[279] http://www.nytimes.com/2014/04/09/us/led-by-stanfords-5-top-colleges-acceptance-rates-hit-new-lows.html?_r=0.

[280] Ibid.

[281] E. H. Erikson, *Identity: Youth and Crisis*. (New York, W. W. Norton, 1968), 87.

[282] Ibid.

else;"[283] and the second as "not definite or made clear; indefinite in form or extent,"[284] and as synonymous with indistinct, undetermined and vague.[285] For our purposes, it is most noteworthy that these terms are *not* representative of adolescents' intrinsic developmental agenda. From this perspective, it is clear that widespread conditions of "educational conformity" run counter to *all* adolescents' fundamental need to search for their own identities, to strive for "distinctness" and to define themselves. Regrettably, within these fiercely competitive conditions, too many students are seen as "indistinguishable"[286] from one another, as they are too often discouraged from exploring, and, therefore, are deprived of opportunities to discover their own unique interests and talents ... all important characteristics of who they might want to be. This is the monoculture effect in action.

Recall from chapter 4 that F. S. Michaels describes a socioeconomic monoculture as a set of "dominant ideas" that form a "governing pattern that a culture obeys" that ultimately "shrinks diversity."[287] Because of this fiercely competitive environment, high-achieving secondary school students and educators have become a monoculture that has, uniformly, "accepted its definition of reality [and has allowed it to become the] invisible foundation that structures and shapes [their] lives."[288]

Because of today's precarious economy, there is an ever-increasing connection between credentials and jobs. For young students everywhere, credentialing has become paramount to everything else, perhaps even paramount to their health and development, and to what Socrates described as "the best possible state of [their] souls."[289] Essentially, within this monoculture, proper credentials translate to the perception of future job security, or to what Lucy Hornby-Reuters calls "a passport to a better life."[290]

Perpetuating all this, as Deresiewicz points out, is the fact that "we're into the second generation now."[291] Further, Deresiewicz reports, "The parents of the kids who have been going through the system since the early

---

[283] Merriam-webster.com.

[284] thefreedictionary.com.

[285] Merriam-webster.com.

[286] http://www.nytimes.com/2014/04/09/us/led-by-stanfords-5-top-colleges-acceptance-rates-hit-new-lows.html?_r=0.

[287] Michaels, *Monoculture*, 1.

[288] Ibid., 2.

[289] http://www.mesacc.edu/~davpy35701/text/plato-apology.html, #14.

[290] Hornby-Reuters, "International Schools in China."

[291] Deresiewicz, *Excellent Sheep*, 35.

1990s are products, increasingly, of the system themselves. People who sent their children to the most selective colleges in the 1970s and '80s were much more likely to have gone to less prestigious, often public, universities, or not to have gone to college at all. Now we're dealing with a cohort of meritocratic professionals for whom a different sort of life is inconceivable."[292]

292 Ibid.

CHAPTER 7

Parents' Voices: The Making of a Perfect Storm

In an effort to more fully complete this discussion, and to include the perspectives of this "cohort of meritocratic professionals," I have also interviewed hundreds of parents associated with independent, international and public schools from within the United States and abroad, with the exact same questions from the *Immunity to Change* paradigm. Not surprisingly, parents the world over admitted to a similarly weighty bind. As these parents considered the same manifestations of their children's stress—anxiety, depression, sleep deprivation, substance abuse, self-injury, and suicidal tendencies—and were asked to identify their own underlying commitments, or the values they held that led to concerns about their children's stress in the first place, these parents quickly identified their baseline commitments and values.

Language of Commitment

Like the educators before them, I asked parents to complete the following statement:

> **"In light of these observed student problems, I am, or we as parents are, committed to the value or the importance of:"**

- Being there for our children
- Supporting them any way we can

- Trying to raise confident and competent kids who have a sense of worth and dignity in and of themselves
- Helping our children develop a sense of their own self-confidence
- Having healthy children above all else
- Loving our kids no matter what

* Once again, these particular responses represent just a small sample of the total responses I gathered from parents over the past three years. While I have listed relatively few responses here, they reflect the sentiments of the majority of parent participants.

As with the educators' responses, you can hear and feel the parents' caring and sincerity, and the earnestness in their spontaneous responses to this initial prompt. These sentiments reflect not only these parents' "baseline commitments/values," but more fundamentally, their fervent commitments to the long-term endeavor of trying to raise healthy, happy, and well-educated children. Most, if not all, parents feel an intense connection with their children, and from that perspective, care deeply about their children's health and well-being. In fact, it is from this instinctive perspective that these parents react with such concern about their children's level of stress. One parent e-mailed this to me:

> Over the past two months, Haden has been swamped with schoolwork. He has been going to sleep at 2 or 3 a.m. and waking up at 6:30 a.m. to rush to school. I have spoken to his advisor and to some of his teachers, and they have noticed that Haden has been too tired and unable to focus. As you know, Haden is planning to apply early decision to [a highly selective college]. I have told Haden's advisor and teachers that I am more worried about his health and well-being than his grades. The stress and pressure are just too much.

Parents' concerns about their children's stress are genuine. As another parent reported, "When my son is suffering, I am suffering. I can't not feel that." However, what many parents may not recognize are the various ways in which they—the parents themselves—actually contribute to their children's stress.

Naming the Barriers

In the "Naming the Barriers" phase of the interview, I asked the parents the same question I had asked previously of the educators:

"In light of your commitment to 'trying to raise confident and competent kids who have a sense of worth and dignity in and of themselves' or to 'loving your kids no matter what,' what are you actually doing, or not doing, at home that gets in the way of, or that interferes with that particular commitment?"

Remarkably, under the same cloak of anonymity, parents admitted:

- We pressure our kids to excel.
- We nag them all the time.
- We expect too-high standards from them.
- We blame them for their mistakes.
- We don't really listen to their complaints.
- We don't respect their priorities.
- We compare our children against each other.
- We pressure them by the example of our own success.
- We overfocus on their academic performance.
- We don't let them listen to their own bodies.
- We micromanage their lives.
- We criticize them for not getting their work done, for spending too much time on social media, and for not getting to bed on time.
- We constantly talk about where they're applying to college.
- We expect them to accomplish everything perfectly.
- We (here it is again) overschedule them.

When asked to more deeply explore their binds, these parents openly acknowledged their own competing commitments, or "those commitments they have to *not* feeling the anxiety that accompanies the contradictory binds they're in."

Mining the Fears

Similarly, I posed the same "Mining the Fears" question to the parents:

"Imagine yourselves trying to do the opposite" of these negative practices, and to try to identify "the most uncomfortable, worrisome or outright scary feelings that would come up" for you.[293]

To this challenging question, similar to how the educators had responded, the parents' candid responses reflected their sudden feelings of anxiety and fear as they stated:

- Society would judge me as a failing parent.
- They wouldn't be competitive in the college process, and we would have failed them.
- I would feel like a failure as a parent.
- I'd feel disappointed with myself as a parent ... that I didn't do everything I could to help my kid.
- I'd fail as a mother.
- I'd be seen as a failure parent, that I didn't fulfill my responsibility as a parent, that I didn't guide my child appropriately.
- I'd be seen as an incompetent parent.
- I'd be a failure in my life's most important job.
- I would feel like such a failure ... that I would have done a horrible job as a parent ... I'd be ashamed of myself.

As a parent, it doesn't get more basic or more personal than that. Poignantly, in her recent book, *How to Raise an Adult: Break Free of the Overparenting Trap and Prepare Your Kid for Success*, [294] Julie Lythcott-Haims openly admits, "I love my kids as fiercely as any parent does, and I know that love is the foundation for all we do as parents. But in my years of researching this book I've learned that many of our behaviors also stem from fears; perhaps chief among them is the fear that our kids won't be successful out in the world. Of course it's natural for parents to want their kids to succeed, but based on research, interviews with more than a hundred

---

[293] Kegan and Lahey, *Immunity to Change*, 238.
[294] Lythcott-Haims, *How to Raise an Adult*.

people, and my own personal experiences, I've come to the conclusion that we define success too narrowly. And what's worse, this narrow, misguided definition of success has led us to harm a generation of young adults—our children."[295] As Lythcott-Haims declares further, "I understand that the systemic problem of over-parenting is rooted in our worries about the world and about how our children will be successful in it without us. Still, we're doing harm. For our kids' sakes, and also for our own, we need to stop parenting from fear and bring a more healthy—a more wisely loving—approach back into our communities, schools and homes."

Where does all this information leave us? What are we to conclude? Essentially, it seems safe to say that we're all in this quandary together. One hundred and fifty years ago, no one saw this coming. What began then as an "old aristocratic" model has gradually become a fiercely competitive, and therefore an increasingly dangerous, meritocratic model that has simultaneously compromised our professional efforts as educators *and* our instinctive mission as parents. Alarmingly, not knowing how else to manage this predicament, we have conceded to these intensifying conditions. Consequently, in our individual and collective efforts to cope, we have unwittingly conducted ourselves in ways that have made the pressure on our students even worse. Our students describe it with words ("The pressure is immense!") and manifest it with their compromised health and behavior (anxiety, depression, sleep deprivation, substance abuse, eating disorders, self-injury, and suicide). Educators admit to overscheduling and overworking their students, and to expecting their students to act and think like adults before they even have that capacity. Finally, parents admit to criticizing, blaming, comparing, and expecting too much of their children. With everyone saying the same thing, like tempestuous forces swirling together, today's "dangerous meritocratic model" seems to have become a "perfect storm" of pressure that renders our students—those who are the very purpose of our work—vulnerable and defenseless.

In our shared efforts to educate and provide for our teenagers as effectively as we can, and as Julie Lythcott-Haims clearly articulates, we seem to have gone too far. We have put the educational cart before the developmental horse and, in so doing, have lost sight of key aspects of our most important responsibility: to foster our teenagers' healthy growth and development, which includes their sound and balanced education. Not

---

[295] Ibid., 1.

only is *that* what our students expect of us, *that* is what we, their educators and their parents, collectively, at our most basic human level, want to give them. It is time for us to reclaim our primary mission "to meet students where they are," "to educate our students in healthy and balance ways," "to have healthy children above all else," and "to love our kids no matter what" before this perfect storm gets any worse.

CHAPTER 8

Students or Schools: Who's Expected to Change?

It's ironic that when students exhibit signs of difficulty in school—when they're showing signs of stress, anxiety, or depression; when they're struggling with organizational and planning abilities and with a variety of other "executive functions;" or even if they're displaying symptoms of either learning or attentional disorders, we expect *them* to change. Rarely, if ever, do we expect *schools* to change. There are plenty of books out there on how to help students make the changes they need in order to adapt to their schools' expectations and demands. *Smart Kids with School Problems*, by Priscilla Vail,[296] is a great example of this kind of book. In her book, Vail expertly highlights that "anger, fear, self-doubt, frustration and pressure [are] reactions that intensify when an intelligent student has a school problem."[297] Further, Vail refers to these intelligent students as those who have "high though hidden intellectual potential"[298] and she calls them "conundrum kids."[299] Finally, Vail states, "The long-term implications of being a conundrum kid are exhilarating whenever [their] talent and self-respect are kept alive."[300] While Vail writes about these "smart kids with school problems" from her many years of experience as a learning specialist, diagnostician, teacher, leader of teacher-training, and as a parent, she still maintains the unspoken assumption that it is the students who need to change—yes,

---

[296] Priscilla Vail, *Smart Kids with School Problems* (New York, Plume Publishers, 1989).
[297] Ibid, preface.
[298] Ibid.
[299] Ibid.
[300] Ibid.

with the wise and guided instruction of skilled teachers, counselors, and learning specialists—but *not* that the schools also need to change.

I am reminded of another change dynamics model, that of individual psychotherapy and its relationship to family psychotherapy. In that model, all too often, individuals (usually one of the children) within a particular family exhibit signs of difficulty: they get anxious or depressed, or they show anger problems and may even get diagnosed with oppositional defiant disorder. In a variety of ways, these kids become the identified patient in need of treatment within the family. Once again, there is tremendous irony in the fact that the family members who have actively contributed to how this "patient" has developed, those who have modeled various ways of handling their emotions and/or expressions of anger management, those with whom this "patient" has developed and reinforced close interpersonal dynamics, are *not* involved with the therapy. You may ask, "How can this be?" Most mental health therapists would agree that the most effective therapy for these individuals—usually children and adolescents—is a combination of individual counseling for them (to consider their own emotional and behavioral patterns) and family therapy (to explore, collectively, how these dynamics have developed within the family, and, particularly, how the family can work together toward establishing and practicing new ways of interacting with each other that reflect healthier and more adaptive functioning).

In light of what educators and parents have reported consistently throughout this book, it seems imperative that we try to change now. We began chapter 6 with a collective acknowledgment that none of us wants "to hyperschool our students and risk disturbing their otherwise healthy development." Having more thoroughly explored the history and context of these concerns, in an effort to begin making good on our similarly collective commitments to "teaching our students in healthy and balanced ways" and to "having healthy children, above all else," we return to Leo Tolstoy's famous question, "What then must we do?"[301]

How to Think about Changing

> "You must be the change you wish to see in the world."
> Mahatma Gandhi

---

[301] Tolstoy, *What Is to Be Done.*

It is worth stating that if the changes necessary for "teaching our students in healthy and balanced ways" and for "having healthy children, above all else" were that easy to make, we certainly would have made them already. Further, in recognition of the decades of "overscheduling and overworking" our students, and of the fiercely competitive conditions that not only have characterized the "incredibly demanding and sometimes unforgiving lifestyle"[302] but that have led to our developing these negative practices in the first place, it is reasonable to expect that the changes we now must make will not happen overnight. Finally, in situations like this one, where what is needed is more of a sea change in how we operate—a systemic transformation—if we hasten to make little changes too quickly, we risk not changing at all.

Consider the reactions of several of the educators who participated in my adapted *Immunity to Change* interview. Because of the integrity with which they responded to the interview prompts, many experienced a series of "aha" moments, or sudden flashes of thinking, "Oh my gosh, I've never thought of it that way!" Further, many of those moments were not only intriguing for these adults, but, also, they seemed uncomfortable in some way, as if unsettled by twinges of sadness and frustration. For example, one administrator commented, "It's just really sad. We really do want to help our students to develop a holistic sense of success focused on a balanced curriculum and meaningful connections with others, but as we relentlessly compress too much activity into an inadequate number of hours every day, and as we demand so much work from our students so much of the time, we actively prohibit that holistic sense of success from even having a chance!"

Another educator acknowledged her frustration after completing the interview as she said, "It's a shame, really, that while we try to be committed to our students' balanced lives, to their wellness of mind and body, we also overschedule them with curricular, extra-curricular and homework activity, and we *never* make time for their downtime, so we constantly expect too much of them and *that* leaves them no choice but to function like robots. I think many students are just going through the motions in this school, so their sense of self seems determined more by external markers of success ... such as their grades and where they get in to college." Still another educator admitted, "While I recognize that I should be worried about our reputation as a rigorous school, I actually am not! In fact, I deeply

---

[302] Cookson and Hodges-Persell, *Preparing for Power*, 20.

believe that, in terms of the school day, 'less would be more' for our students and also for our school. I think the 'how' at this school is more important than the 'what.'" Finally, another educator completed the interview and stated, "Actually, I've thought a lot about these issues and have come to believe, strongly, that if we made some of these changes, and if we actually addressed these problems, then we'd be a *better* school; that we'd be known as a great school that has 'figured it out,' and not as a school that has failed or lost its rigor. I can see a way out—not the traditional path—that will make us better."

David Elkind: A Voice of Reason

When psychologist and author David Elkind wrote *The Hurried Child: Growing Up Too Fast Too Soon* in 1981, he warned of "the dangers of exposing our children to overwhelming pressures that can lead to a wide range of childhood and teenage crises."[303] Over time, Elkind published several editions of this groundbreaking book because what it meant for children to be "hurried" in subsequent years kept changing dramatically since his initial publication. Twenty-five years later, in 2006, Elkind published a twenty-fifth anniversary edition in which he provided a "new commentary to put a quarter century of trends and change into perspective for parents today."[304] Most importantly, in that twenty-fifth anniversary edition, Elkind wrote, "In our information society, the brain has become, at least for parents and educators, the ultimate scientific authority."[305]

As I finish writing this book in 2016, ten years after Elkind's twenty-fifth anniversary edition, so much has changed again. Consider one of the obvious—and constant—changes: advances in technology. According to Cris Rowan, columnist for *Huffington Post*, "Advances in technology have had an impact on the 21st century family [that are] fracturing its very foundation, and causing a disintegration of core values that long ago were the fabric that held families together."[306] To be sure, children and adolescents of today are faced with very different challenges than most parents recall about their own childhoods. For example, as high school students, while

---

[303] http://www.amazon.com/The-Hurried-Child-Growing-Edition.
[304] Ibid.
[305] Elkind, *The Hurried Child*, 108.
[306] http://www.huffingtonpost.com/cris-rowan/technology-children-negative-impact_b_3343245.html.

we may have faced some of our own distraction challenges, none of us carried cell phones in our pockets, so we weren't subject to the nonstop and pervasive distractions that such "advances" have posed to all high school students today, distractions that have been characterized by students experiencing "continuous partial attention."[307] This term, coined by Linda Stone in 1998, described students as "paying partial attention ... continuously ... motivated by a desire not to miss anything, a state in which attention is on a priority or primary task, while, at the same time, scanning for other people, activities, or opportunities, and replacing the primary task with something that seems, in this next moment, more important."[308]

While Elkind wrote poignantly about many aspects of childhood that had changed or that had been "hurried" by anxious adults, in the context of that twenty-fifth anniversary edition discussion, Elkind also cited other aspects of childhood—and for our purposes, adolescence—that have remained the same. For example, Elkind reminded us, "It still takes a mother nine months to carry a baby to term. The ages at which children learn to walk, talk, and learn the three Rs have not changed, even with all the effort to introduce them earlier. Parents are still the major influence on children's overall development, and children still need our love, our support, and our limit-setting."[309]

For an example that is relevant to adolescence, consider the onset of puberty. For all children throughout history and around the entire world, puberty begins typically between the ages of eleven and fourteen years when their pituitary glands begin to secrete hormones that trigger a series of sexual maturity features and that stimulate a long process of their developing into adult men and women. Except in some rare medical conditions, the timing of puberty's onset—and therefore of the onset of one's associated physical, cognitive, and social-emotional development—is naturally determined and cannot be "hurried." This biologically determined reality is unmistakably evident as each new group of ninth-graders arrives to school. Typically, some ninth-graders look like eleventh- and twelfth-graders, while others still look like seventh- and sixth-graders.

This distribution of developmentally-different-but-same-aged kids, combined with the hundreds of disclosures from adults from all around

---

[307] https://lindastone.net/qa/continuous-partial-attention/.

[308] https://lindastone.net/2009/11/30/beyond-simple-multi-tasking-continuous-partial-attention/.

[309] http://www.parentbooksummaries.com/the-hurried-child-25th-anniversary-edition.

the world, helps us to appreciate that in spite of our efforts to design a picture-perfect education that provides our children with a "passport to a better life,"[310] we may be overdoing it and putting some of our students at risk. We seem to be forgetting that although many of our students look like adults, speak like adults, and even try to act like adults, they are *not* adults: they are early adolescents with their own developmental integrity. In fact, and surprising as this may seem, *every* student at *every* independent, international and public secondary school throughout the world is an adolescent, typically between the ages of fourteen and eighteen years, whose physical, cognitive, and social-emotional capacities are still wholly developing. Furthermore, our unintended but still-deliberate efforts to augment our students' status by overscheduling, overworking, and, in some cases, overwhelming them in our hyperschooling milieu[311] threatens their very development.

Schedule Changes

Interestingly, a few high performance secondary schools have already made developmentally appropriate changes that have had positive, measureable effects. For example, one school initiated its own independent research to examine the effects of a delayed school start time on its students. Specifically, this school delayed the start of school from 8:00 a.m. to 8:30 a.m. for a period of two months, and the results were stunning. By the end of this two-month study, "the mean school night sleep duration increased by 45 minutes, and average bedtime advanced by 18 minutes; the percentage of students getting less than 7 hours of sleep decreased by 79.4%, and those reporting at least 8 hours of sleep increased from 16.4% to 54.7%. Students reported significantly more satisfaction with sleep and experienced improved motivation. Daytime sleepiness, fatigue, and depressed mood were all reduced. Furthermore, many health-related variables, including health center visits for fatigue-related complaints, and class attendance also improved."[312] At the conclusion of this two-month

---

[310] A. Rosenfeld and N. Wise, *Hyper-Parenting: The Overscheduled Child* (http://www.hyper-parenting.com/paper.htm).

[311] Ibid.

[312] J. A. Owens, K. Belon, and P. Moss, "Impact of Delaying School Start Time on Adolescent Sleep, Mood, and Behavior," *Arch Pediatr Adolesc Med.* 164, no. 7 (2010):608–14 (doi:10.1001/archpediatrics.2010.96).

study, this particular school implemented the thirty-minute delayed start as a permanent change.

Of note, a more recent study by the American Academy of Pediatrics in 2014 reinforced the findings of this two-month study and found "evidence that strongly implicates earlier school start times (i.e., before 8:30 a.m.) as a key modifiable contributor to insufficient sleep."[313] Furthermore, at the time of this writing, "a substantial body of research has now demonstrated that delaying school start times is an effective countermeasure to chronic sleep loss and has a wide range of potential benefits to students with regard to physical and mental health, safety, and academic achievement. The American Academy of Pediatrics strongly supports the efforts of school districts to optimize sleep in students and urges high schools and middle schools to aim for start times that allow students the opportunity to achieve optimal levels of sleep (8.5–9.5 hours) and to improve physical (e.g., reduced obesity risk) and mental (e.g., lower rates of depression) health, safety (e.g., drowsy driving crashes), academic performance, and quality of life."[314]

Another school spent about thirty years gradually revamping its schedule. At the outset, "largely in response to a student who left the school and wrote to the faculty about the pace of life,"[315] this particular school, a boarding school that had maintained a six-day per week class schedule (yes, weekly Saturday classes) for many, many years, endeavored in the early 1980s to reduce the number of Saturdays by experimenting with an every other Saturday schedule. As one of this school's administrators recalled, "After a decade of every-other Saturday, in the '90s, we began to pull back even more on Saturday classes, largely due to both standardized testing and faculty discontent with them. We probably had four [Saturday class days] each term. Then, late in the '90s, we got rid of Saturday classes during the winter term as a means to get kids healthier during the sicker months. Sleep was more important than the sacred Saturday classes. In the early 2000s, we seemed to drift even further away from Saturday classes. We had maybe three in the fall and three in the spring terms. Then, in the summer of 2013, the administrators decided as a team to eliminate them altogether. No fanfare. Just eliminated. We have had two years without them."[316] It is worth emphasizing here that while this particular school has made this

---

[313] http://pediatrics.aappublications.org/content/early/2014/08/19/peds.2014-1697.

[314] Ibid.

[315] Anonymous administrator.

[316] Ibid.

gradual but significant schedule change to accommodate both students' basic health needs *and* the "faculty's discontent," it has simultaneously maintained its reputation and brand as a rigorous and selective school that *continues* to "get kids into the most selective colleges."

It is striking that one school made a significant schedule change after only a two-month study, while another one made a similar schedule change, gradually, over a period of about thirty years. As we review these changes, two important factors stand out. First, and perhaps most important, both of these changes reflect changes to those schools' schedules. In light of our earlier realization that practically *every* educator and parent interviewed for this book revealed that "overscheduling our students" remains one of the primary practices, in *every* school, which interferes with their otherwise genuine commitment to "educating [their] students in healthy and balanced ways," these two schools have certainly recognized and have taken action to address the problems associated with their own histories of overscheduling. The second important factor that stands out from these changes is that neither of these schools suffered any loss either to its reputation or to its college admissions statistics. In fact, it is arguable that both schools enjoyed an ever better reputation and became even more desirable to applicants and their parents specifically because of these schedule adjustments that actively accommodated their students' developmental sleep needs.

Without a doubt, these developmentally minded changes, whether they took two months or thirty years to accomplish, are to be celebrated as the very kind of changes that competitive schools everywhere now need to make. As we have just seen, even minor changes in these two schools' frenetic schedules have had noticeable and healthy effects. Enabling students to get more sleep and impacting their ability to reduce their depressed mood and/or decrease their health center visits are all undeniable improvements about which these schools should be pleased.

At this time, you may be asking, "Is that it? Is a minor schedule change all we need to do to resolve these challenges?" To that question, my unambiguous response is, "No!" While these schedule adjustments help us to confirm that "overscheduling our students" is, indeed, one of our schools' most developmentally compromising features, it is certainly not the only one. Recall that educators and parents have all admitted that in addition to overscheduling their students, they also assign students with too much work; expect them, prematurely, to act and think like adults; and overemphasize students' achievement more than their effort. In an effort to grasp the totality of how our "negative but widespread practices" may be compromising our students' overall development, consider these well-known effects of the other ways in which we admit to having mistreated them.

Too Much Work and Associated Sleep Deprivation

We admit to assigning our students with too much work. It is striking that many *adults* who report feeling overworked *in their jobs* relate not only experiences of psychological and emotional distress, but also a reduction in their overall levels of well-being.[317] Further, these negative effects are reported as being more severe when these *adults* feel both overworked and powerless, or increasingly helpless in the face of constant work demands.[318] If these are the effects of feeling overworked that *adults* experience, do we think that our adolescents will somehow be immune to them?

As we discussed in chapter 5, recent brain imaging studies have confirmed that because all adolescents are still developing, their brains are even more vulnerable to ongoing environmental stressors. From this perspective, we can conclude that the developmental cost of overworking our students is, indeed, a pricey one. In addition, one of the most common effects of our assigning too much work—in an already overscheduled milieu—is our students' chronic sleep deprivation. Accordingly, the American Academy of Pediatrics has recognized insufficient sleep in adolescents as a public health issue that significantly affects their health and safety, as well as their academic success.[319] In light of these realities, it is well-known that many *adults* manifest feelings of being overworked with symptoms such as fatigue, compromised memory, anxiety, depression, greater susceptibility to illness, a tendency to rely on alcohol or other drugs for relaxation, and strained social relationships.[320] Sadly, these "adult" symptoms are also recognizable as common and recurring symptoms among many of our students, too.

---

[317] Remus Ilies, Nikolaos Dimotakis, and Irene E. De Pater, "Psychological and Physiological Reactions to High Workloads: Implications for Well-Being, *Personnel Psychology* 63, no, 2 (12 May 2010):407–36.

[318] Ibid.

[319] http://pediatrics.aappublications.org/content/early/2014/08/19/peds.2014-1697.

[320] http://www.ehow.com/info_8135341_signs-overworked.html.

Chronological vs. Developmental Age

We admit to expecting our students to act and think like adults before they have those capacities. As discussed in chapter 3, this "negative but widespread practice" constitutes one of the most common developmental errors adults make in their interactions and dealings with adolescents.[321] Recall Kegan's warning: "If adults mistake [adolescents'] physiology and/or [their] verbal ability for [their] psychological age,"[322] and then expect those adolescents to function as if they're actually young adults, then it's the *adults* who "create a situation which is dangerous for both themselves and for the developmentally delayed teenager."[323] As Kegan asserted further, "The cost to a person of being unseen, of being seen as the person-one-might-become rather than the person-one-is,"[324] is a "bewildering experience of being unfairly demanded of."[325]

Once again, similar to when they're being overscheduled and/or overworked, when our adolescent students are "unseen" for whom they actually are, and instead, are "seen" and, therefore, expected to function like "persons-they-might-become," it is a developmental setup. While many adolescents feel flattered, initially, by these grand adult expectations, they cannot sustain that adult level of functioning because they just don't have the developmental capacity and readiness to do so. As these expectations continue, and as students keep trying to meet them, they show ever-increasing signs of stress: fatigue, anxiety, and depression, and the now-familiar cluster of behavioral manifestations including eating disorders, self-harm/cutting, substance abuse, and suicidal gestures. Without a doubt, *these* are the developmental costs of "being unseen": *these* are the "bewildering experiences of being unfairly demanded of."[326]

Achievement vs. Effort

We admit to overemphasizing our students' achievements more than their efforts. In some ways, this may be our most developmentally compromising

---

[321] Kegan, *The Evolving Self*, 178.
[322] Ibid.
[323] Ibid.
[324] Ibid.
[325] Ibid., 179.
[326] Ibid.

practice. In our well-intended efforts to recognize our students' successes, we may, instead, be impeding their growth by depriving them of opportunities to learn and develop necessary academic, social, and executive skills. Consider how our emphasis on achievement instead of effort often plays out.

First of all, as Devlin mentioned in chapter 3, "there is just crazy competition ... having heard from like freshman year on, that we have to build up our resumes for our college applications." Devlin recalled, "Kids wanted various positions—not because they were passionate about them—but because they would look good on a resume." Our emphasis on high achievement for all students necessarily pits them against each other as rivals, forcing them into competition for the same achievement credentials.

Second, our emphasis on our students' high achievement—and not on their efforts—perpetuates a "pressure not to fail."[327] For many students, ironically, short-term efforts to avoid failure can actually interfere with their long-term ambition for true success. Recent advances in neuroimaging have shown, unmistakably, that avoiding struggle and failure can deprive individuals of important skill development—for *any* skill—including athletic skills, music skills, academic skills, and even executive functioning skills.

In his recent book, *The Talent Code*, Daniel Coyle asserts, "struggle is not optional—it's neurologically required"[328] for the most effective learning to occur. Coyle introduces the concept of "deep practice,"[329] or "mistake-focused practice,"[330] as "struggling in certain targeted ways, operating at the edges of your ability, where you make mistakes [in order to] make you smarter."[331] In stark contrast to the emphasis on credentials and achievement, Coyle emphasizes "experiences where you're forced to slow down, make errors, and correct them"[332] as the ones that lead to genuine learning and success.

Coyle's *The Talent Code* focuses on the elegant biological role of myelin—the fatty membrane that insulates neuronal axons—in *all* skill

---

[327] http://www.alfiekohn.org/article/costs-overemphasizing-achievement/.

[328] D. Coyle, *The Talent Code: Greatness Isn't Born. It's Grown. Here's How.* (New York, Bantam Books, 2009), 42.

[329] Ibid.,18.

[330] Ibid., 34.

[331] Ibid., 18.

[332] Ibid.

development. As Coyle points out, "Every human movement, thought, or feeling is a precisely timed electric signal traveling through a chain of neurons—a circuit of fibers. Further, myelin wraps these nerve fibers and increases signal strength, speed and accuracy. The more we fire a particular circuit, the more myelin optimizes that circuit, and the stronger, faster, and more fluent our movements and thoughts become."[333] "All skill is myelin insulation that wraps neural circuits and that grows according to certain signals,"[334] and the only way to fire these signals is to act, to do something! Essentially, the more we practice any skill (or thought, or feeling or movement, etc.) the more myelin we develop on the neurons associated with that skill, and the more we reinforce and develop it. Coyle promotes "deep practice," also called "mistake-focused practice"[335] as the optimal way to learn. In "deep practice," Coyle notes, we "fire the circuit, attend to mistakes, then fire it again, over and over."[336] From this perspective, Coyle asserts, "struggle is not optional—it's neurologically required."[337] For many of our students, our overemphasis on their achievements—and not on their efforts—may deprive them of the true learning that only their repeated efforts—deep practice—can provide.

Perhaps you can now appreciate that making a minor adjustment to our frenetic schedules would be just that—a minor adjustment—to our otherwise established system of unhealthy but widespread practices. Although a schedule change might, in fact, lead to improved sleep patterns and physically healthier students, it would not necessarily address students' psychological and emotional distress from being overworked; it would not address students' "bewildering" costs from being both "unseen" and "unfairly demanded of"; nor would it address the reality that overemphasizing students' achievement may actually deprive them of otherwise ongoing efforts to practice, and eventually hardwire, a whole cluster of academic, social-emotional, and executive functioning skills they will need throughout their lives. Each one of these other conditions reflects just one part of our now-established *system* of unhealthy but widespread practices, itself a whole set of developmental errors that we commit, commonly overlook, and perpetuate. Furthermore, it may now be clearer that our reworking

[333] Ibid., 32.
[334] Ibid., 33.
[335] Ibid., 34.
[336] Ibid.
[337] Ibid., 42.

and revising just one of these conditions—such as the schedule—would not mean that we would have reworked and revised them all. To do that, we would have to prioritize respecting accurate and current knowledge of adolescent development before we teach, coach, or advise, much as medical doctors must prioritize accurate and current knowledge of the human body before they diagnose, prescribe, or operate.

It is compelling that the Shanghai Education Commission has already begun to contemplate these changes. In spite of their being "the top-performing school system according to the latest PISA tables,"[338] the Shanghai schools are "less impressed by [their] own performance than everyone else seems to be."[339] Reportedly, "Yi Houqin, a high-ranking official in the Shanghai Education Commission, recently said that he was pleased but not surprised at how well their students had done. After all, the system is focused on drilling them in rote learning to succeed in just these sorts of tests. That is not the point. [Houkin] said that the Commission was considering stepping away from PISA testing at some point. 'Shanghai does not need so-called #1 schools,' he said. 'What it needs are schools that follow sound educational principles, respect principles of students' physical and psychological development, and lay a solid foundation for students' lifelong development.'"[340]

---

[338] Robinson and Aronica, *Creative Schools*, 19.
[339] Ibid.
[340] Ibid.

CHAPTER 9

Questions to Ask Ourselves!

As we near the end of this book, I invite you to consider a few closing questions:

1. Independent and international school websites advertise their schools as educational communities in which they interweave mutual respect and compassion for others with their unwavering efforts to develop students' keen and creative minds, their healthy bodies and their moral character … all as they strive to help students reach their full academic potential. Ironically, while these websites reflect clearly what these schools say they do, as we have collectively acknowledged throughout this book—and for reasons we have courageously identified—they don't fully reflect what else is going on. In light of what so many educators and parents have candidly acknowledged, how can we now deliver on what we publicly promise?

2. In chapter 3, we acknowledged that in today's increasingly competitive environment, our students are too frequently "unseen" for who they actually are and, instead, are treated as "persons-they-might-become." Further, we have also just acknowledged that for *all* our students—even for our many "successful" ones—their "being unseen" is a direct consequence of *our* recurring developmental errors that set them up for fatigue, anxiety, and depression, and for a variety of troubling behavioral manifestations. How can we now respond to these increasingly alarming conditions? How can we align our teaching, coaching and advising with what David

Elkind called "the ultimate scientific authority," the developing human brain?

3. As this book has helped us to acknowledge, we seem to have been keeping our own anxieties at bay by perpetuating a whole system of "negative but widespread practices" that, unfortunately, are detrimental to our students' development. In light of this decades-old conflict, how can we now begin to make changes that both respect adolescent development *and* that simultaneously help us to address our own fears?

One of these questions is about our truth in advertising; one is about aligning our educational practices with our students' developmental capacities, and one is about trying to do all of this in ways that simultaneously help us to deal with our own anxieties—our previously unacknowledged fears that led us to developing these negative practices in the first place.

Adaptive vs. Technical Challenges

Clearly, these questions present us with enormous challenges for which no easy answers exist. Until this point, the *Immunity to Change* paradigm has provided us with an effective diagnostic structure that has enabled us to unearth these binds. Further, while the *Immunity to Change* offers helpful guidelines for how we might now work on resolving our binds, it does *not* do the work of actually changing: that work is for us, and us alone, to do. As we consider trying to address these enormous challenges, we may take some comfort from guiding principles proposed by another change theorist, Ronald Heifetz, who has been down this road before, and has both researched and practiced widely in the field of organizational change.

In his book *Leadership without Easy Answers*, Heifetz writes about change in ways that can be helpful to us now. Fortunately, Heifetz acknowledges that "many problems are embedded in complicated and interactive systems,"[341] a fact that certainly resonates with us. Truthfully, within the context of our own "complicated and interactive systems," we never would have imagined overlooking our students' developmental capacities. However, as we have seen throughout this book, our anxious efforts to

---

[341] R. Heifetz, *Leadership without Easy Answers* (Cambridge, MA., Belknap Press of Harvard University Press, 1994), 2.

cope with intensifying economic and cultural conditions, over time, have resulted in our unintentionally doing so.

Heifetz has worked with a wide range of groups and organizations from government, business, health care, education, law, the military, and the clergy. As a result of his many years of teaching and consulting within these varied groups, Heifetz has developed a "general theory that has practical application"[342] for how we might now consider our own process of change. Specifically, Heifetz makes "a key distinction between *adaptive* and *technical* problems," a distinction "that points to different modes of action required to deal with routine problems, in contrast with those that demand innovation and learning."[343]

In Heifetz's framework, *adaptive* problems refer to those problems for which "no adequate response has yet been developed."[344] For these kinds of problems, Heifetz notes, "No organizational response can be called into play that will clearly resolve [them]; no clear expertise can be found, no single sage has general credibility, no established procedure will suffice. Stresses build up and produce a sense of urgency, and in these situations, our inclination to look to authority may generate inappropriate dependencies."[345] These problems are *adaptive* because "the responsibility for solving them has to be shared"[346]; they "demand innovation and learning"[347] "both to define the problems and implement solutions."[348]

In significant contrast, *technical* problems refer to those problems for which "we know already how to respond."[349] Heifetz asserts that technical problems "are not easy, nor are they unimportant. These problems are *technical* because the necessary knowledge about them already has been digested and put in the form of a legitimized set of known organizational procedures guiding what to do and role authorizations guiding who should do it. For these situations, we turn to authority with reasonable expectations"[350] that *they* will be able to solve them. Typically, these situations require hardly anything of us, only that we hire or engage the right

---

[342] Ibid., 7.
[343] Ibid., 8.
[344] Ibid., 72.
[345] Ibid.
[346] Ibid., 74.
[347] Ibid., 8.
[348] Ibid., 75.
[349] Ibid., 71.
[350] Ibid.

"technician" or expert to solve our problem. Auto mechanics, surgeons, electricians, and airplane pilots—and experts and/or consultants of all kinds—are great examples of the kind of authority figures who follow "digested and already-legitimized sets of known procedures" to guide us to so-called technical solutions.

Heifetz asserts further that in many situations, neither individuals nor organizations "are inclined to differentiate between *adaptive* and *technical* work."[351] More commonly, "the harsher the reality, the harder we look to authority for a remedy that saves us from [the work of] adjustment. By and large, we want answers, not questions. Even the toughest individual [and organization] tends to avoid realities that require *adaptive* work, searching instead for an authority ... to provide the way out."[352]

Ironically, within the context of our competitive schools, for over twenty years, I have been what Heifetz would call such an "authority." As a clinical psychologist, I was hired many years ago to assess and treat one school's academically and emotionally troubled students. I was not hired to help that school do the work of *adaptive* change. Throughout two decades of this *technical* clinical work in a variety of other schools, I have, indeed, assessed and treated many hundreds of troubled students, and consistent with how I first understood my role, I have encouraged all of these students to adapt and change. I now know, however, that this *technical* approach has been too one-sided.

To their credit, educators have recognized, over time, that too many of their students have developed real and lasting troubles. In addition, these same educators also have responded by allocating what they have believed to be the appropriate, if *technical*, resources—one or two trained counselors and appropriate office spaces—in a sincere effort to relieve their students' troubles. Essentially, by providing access to school-employed counselors, each school has indirectly said to its students, "We offer you these skilled clinicians. Make good use of them to make the changes *you need to make* in order to get back on track here." Like so many other leaders who commonly err in this way,[353] these educators have unwittingly made the mistake of try-ing to solve what you may now recognize as enormous *adaptive* challenges with insufficient *technical* solutions. Don't get me wrong: it is certainly fair

---

[351] Ibid., 76.
[352] Ibid.
[353] Ibid., 75.

to ask students to change. Within the limitations of their developmental capacities, challenging students to make some of these changes can lead to positive growth trajectories. However, if we adults don't also change, if we're not also willing to *adapt* in ways that reflect our sympathetic understanding of who our students really are, then, in the acknowledging words of one administrator, "We are holding kids to an unfair standard."

Let's be very clear: Establishing truth in advertising, aligning our educational practices with our students' developmental capacities, and doing all this in ways that simultaneously help us to deal with our own anxieties constitute enormous *adaptive* challenges for which "no adequate responses have yet been developed," and for which "no clear expertise can be found, no single sage has general credibility, [and] no established procedure will suffice." In addition, as the consistent, if not uniform, testimony of educators, parents, and students has already revealed, "stresses *have* built up and produced a sense of urgency." At this point, "our inclination [may be] to look to authority" to solve our problems, but I can assure you that *that* would be a mistake. Remember: these challenges are *adaptive* because "the responsibility for solving them has to be shared."[354] Furthermore, not only does this responsibility have to be shared *within* individual schools, but, also, competitive schools everywhere need to unite in mutual support of one another, engaging these challenges together.

As mentioned earlier, today's higher education environment has too frequently been described as one big educational arms race. Recall that Gordon Winston of Williams College noted, "The essence of an arms race is *position*—how a country or university stands relative to others. No single institution alone can safely quit the race, even though all institutions, together, would be better off if everyone did."[355] As we have already discussed, this ongoing race for position at the college level translates daily to more extreme competition for our younger and more vulnerable adolescent students, all of whom are then forced to pay an increasingly damaging and developmentally compromising price.

It is worth stating that many of our schools are already familiar with making major, and to some degree, *adaptive* changes. For example, many schools became coeducational during the 1970s; many have changed their

[354] Ibid., 74.
[355] https://net.educause.edu/ir/library/pdf/ffp0103s.pdf (The Positional Arms Race in Higher Education).

admissions approaches, over time, thereby attracting students from different cities and countries around the world so as to admit an increasingly diverse student culture; many have adjusted their curricula to reflect various
educational trends; some, as we have seen, have changed their schedules to
accommodate adolescent sleep needs, and many have changed their physical features by constructing state-of-the-art athletic facilities, integrated
math-science buildings, modern theaters, and spacious libraries. In general,
these kinds of changes confirm for us that making major changes for these
schools is nothing new. While these changes have occurred for various
reasons and at different times, they still reflect the fact that high-achieving
secondary schools everywhere have their own well-documented histories
of having modified key aspects of how they operate that have resulted
in a "new normal" of real and lasting changes. Basically, we have done it
before, and we can do it again. The only question we face now, however, is
this: Are we actually willing to engage *this* adaptive process and, thereby,
commit ourselves to taking responsibility for our own anxieties instead of
projecting them on to our students?

As you may now appreciate, not only are our challenges hugely *adaptive* ones—"no adequate response has yet been developed ... no established
procedure will suffice"[356]—but they are also widespread, if not universal,
challenges in that "the responsibility for solving them has to be shared"[357]
by *all* of us. We *must* work together "to define the problems and implement
solutions,"[358] both within specific schools and in the expansive network of
high-performance secondary schools throughout the world. We owe it to
adolescents everywhere—not to just a few—to understand and respect their
unique developmental capacities—*who they are*—as we strive to educate
them to find their true potential.

[356] Heifetz, *Leadership without Easy Answers*, 72.
[357] Ibid., 74.
[358] Ibid., 75.

CHAPTER 10

Supportive Strategies

As you may recall from this book's introduction, I mentioned that I would not be able to prescribe a list of specific recommendations for how every school could change. Importantly, the details with respect to how each school works to address these challenges can only be determined from within *each school's* unique culture, history, and traditions. However, in this section, I provide a list of "supportive strategies" that, hopefully, will encourage individual schools to consider their own curricular and extra-curricular programs from a developmental perspective, and then prioritize which aspects of adolescent functioning—within their school—might need the most developmental adjustment.

What might it mean for schools to be more developmentally empathic? I hope the following list will offer some helpful guiding principles with which to answer this question.

The Schedule

> "The key is not to prioritize what's on your schedule,
> but to schedule your priorities."[359]
> Stephen Covey

As we have seen throughout this book, one of the most frequently identified problems in these high-performance schools—also called "epicenters

---

[359] S. Covey, *The Seven Habits of Highly Effective People* (New York, Simon & Shuster, anniversary edition, 2013).

of overachievement,"[360] is the over-scheduled nature of students' everyday lives. Most schools admit to adding more and more to students' schedules without ever taking anything away. Given the well-known effects of over-scheduling, such as exhaustion, increased stress, decreased motivation, and experiences of anxiety and possible depression—all of which compromise the students' overall approach to learning—is it possible for schools to create more "downtime" for their students rather than continuing to add more demands to their schedules? Presently, many students experience increasingly frenetic lives of incessant work demands without sufficient time to slow down and unwind, let alone to get the medically determined amount of sleep they need for healthy functioning and development. If our true priorities are "presenting our students with an appropriate balance of challenge and support" and "educating our students in healthy, safe, and balanced ways," then our schedules need to reflect our stated priorities. Admittedly, changing our schedules may be easier said than done, but as we have already seen, making even minor changes can lead to major benefits for many students. Few of us would contest that a more balanced schedule would naturally lead to improved health and wellness for our students.

Sleep

"We are such stuff as dreams are made on; and
our little life is rounded with a sleep."[361]
William Shakespeare

As mentioned above, in a way that is closely tied to the overall schedule; one of the most developmentally empathic ways that schools could change would be to proceed in ways that enable students to get close to the amount of sleep they actually need. While the American Pediatric Association's guidelines for adolescents' sleep of just over nine hours per night may seem like too much to accommodate, *any* changes that enable those students who ordinarily sleep for four to five hours per night – or fewer – would be a great improvement. It is noteworthy that the effects of chronic sleep disorders often mimic the symptoms of ADHD, anxiety, and depression. Consequently, many students who present with these familiar symptoms

---

[360] Bruni, "Best, Brightest—and Saddest."
[361] W. Shakespeare, *The Tempest*, Act 4, Scene 1, 148–58.

are often treated for these other disorders, when the primary cause for their inattentiveness, anxiety, or depressed mood is chronic sleep deprivation.

Developing Executive Functions

> "Executive functions are directive capacities that are responsible
> for a person's ability to engage in purposeful, organized, strategic,
> self-regulated, goal-directed processing of perceptions, emotions,
> thoughts and actions. As a collection of directive capacities,
> executive functions cue the use of other mental capacities."[362]
> George McCloskey

Since we now know, unequivocally, that the prefrontal cortex is the region of the brain most associated with the growth and development of a wide variety of "executive" skills, and that those very skills are in early stages of development during puberty and throughout the adolescent years, it seems only natural that developmentally empathic schools would educate students more directly regarding the executive skills they need most to be successful, especially within such rigorous academic environments.

During the process of researching and writing this book, I met with the administrative and coaching team of Beyond BookSmart,[363] an agency whose sole mission is executive function coaching. I asked if they could provide me with information about the students who are most frequently referred to them and, also, for which executive functions were they most frequently hired to coach. According to their records, the most frequently referred students are ninth- and tenth-graders, most of whom need specialized coaching for what Beyond BookSmart terms, "the big four" executive skills: organizational skills, task initiation, time management, and emotional regulation. No wonder they are called "the big four!" Most adolescents struggle to learn these skills, especially when they are enrolled in "fiercely competitive schools" where the price of failure can be so high. Given the "normal developmental variation" with respect to these skills that we discussed in chapter 4, it makes perfect sense that not *all* ninth- and tenth-graders have mastered these skills, and that most students would benefit from a creative program of executive function instruction that is

---

[362] McCloskey, Perkins, and Van Divner, *Assessment and Intervention*, 15.
[363] www.beyondbooksmart.com.

integrated with, if not tailored to, their specific curricular and extracurricular demands. While "the big four" executive skills are certainly not the only ones needed for success in demanding academic environments, they certainly are essential, as each one of them reflects a key feature of what is typically expected during one of the most sensitive developmental periods of the entire human lifespan.

Mindfulness Meditation

"Work is not always required. There is such a thing as sacred idleness."[364]
George MacDonald

In light of the recent and ongoing upsurge of compelling research on the practice of mindfulness meditation, I would feel remiss not to mention it here as a supportive strategy worth cultivating. Thanks to the work of Dr. Jon Kabat-Zinn, who "developed the Mindfulness Based Stress Reduction (MBSR) program at the University of Massachusetts Medical Center, MBSR has evolved into a common form of complementary medicine addressing a variety of health problems."[365] Further, in addition to the practice of mindfulness meditation in many health-care settings, "mindfulness has become a common part of the curriculum in classrooms around the world."[366] For our purposes, among its many benefits, the practice of mindfulness meditation has been shown by medical and psychological researchers alike to "enhance student wellbeing and help children develop a greater awareness of their body, mind and emotions."[367] Importantly, with this strategy, we do *not* want to add to our students' already-hectic schedules. However, as many schools have already been able to do, developmentally empathic schools could integrate the teaching and practice of mindfulness meditation within their existing curricular or extracurricular programs, even as

---

[364] G. MacDonald, *Lilith* (First published in 1895; reissued by Open Road Media Sci-Fi & Fantasy, September 2014.)

[365] Mindfullivingprogams.com.

[366] K. Ager, N. Albrecht, and P. Cohen, "Mindfulness in Schools Research Project: Exploring Students' Perspectives of Mindfulness—What are students' perspectives of learning mindfulness practices at school?" *Psychology* 6 (2015): 896–914, doi: 10.4236/psych.2015.67088.

[367] Ibid.

an optional "structured downtime" to enhance students' (and educators') overall experience.

Respecting Developmental Integrity

"As kids reach adolescence, they need more than ever that
we watch over them. Adolescence is not about letting go,
it's about hanging on during a very bumpy ride."
Ron Taffel

Recall from chapters 2 and 3 that one of the most common developmental errors that many educators acknowledged in their interactions and dealings with their students was "expecting students to think like adults and behave like adults before they have that skillset," and then treating those adolescents as if they *were* adults. The truth is that many adolescents mislead educators and parents alike with their adult-like appearances and their verbal sophistication such that educators and parents mistakenly treat adolescents as if "they have [adult] skillsets."[368] This is tricky business, for sure, but adults still have a responsibility not to "mistake [adolescents'] physiology and/or [their] verbal ability for [their] psychological age,"[369] and expect those adolescents to function beyond their developmental capacities, as that "creates a situation which is dangerous for both [adults] and for the developmentally delayed teenagers."[370]

While Ron Taffel claims, "As kids reach adolescence, they need more than ever that we watch over them,"[371] this does *not* mean that we smother them and interfere with their need to take on new challenges—and even some risks—along their natural developmental trajectories. Finding the right balance is certainly one of the supportive strategies worth pursuing. For example, all-school reads of books such as Daniel Siegel's *Brainstorm: The Power and Purpose of the Teenage Brain*, or Francis Jensen and Amy Ellis's *The Teenage Brain: A Neuroscientist's Survival Guide to Raising Adolescents and Young Adults*, or John McKinnon's *To Change a Mind: Parenting to Promote Maturity in Teenagers* could spark lively discussions and a series of in-house workshops for educators and parents alike, thereby

[368] Kegan, *The Evolving Self*, 178.
[369] Ibid.
[370] Ibid.
[371] http://casafamilyday.org/blog/2013/05/13/top-parenting-quotes.

promoting ongoing professional development in these important matters. In addition, numerous films, podcasts, and blogs could reinforce and/or illustrate essential developmental concepts. The key here is that educators and parents work *together* in a collective effort *not* to treat adolescents like adults, *not* to put adolescents in roles that belong to adults, and *not* to "create situations which are dangerous for both [adults] and for the developmentally delayed teenagers."[372] Instead, the objective is to take full advantage of the rich information that is now readily available to learn as much as possible about how to actually treat adolescents like adolescents.

Overworking

"Homework: Because seven hours of school wasn't enough!"
Anonymous

This is a delicate issue. It certainly is not up to me to make any real determination with respect to how much homework is either enough or too much. I include this brief section on homework as one of the supportive strategies only as a way of keeping the discussion alive about these important issues, particularly since so many educators who participated in my interviews openly admitted to "assigning too much work." As many readers know, a wide range of opinions already exists regarding the necessity and/or value of homework. I am not engaging that lively debate here, as I recognize—and support—that most competitive secondary schools endorse homework as an essential element of their overall approach to educating their students and preparing them effectively for college. Further, I know that many schools have already deliberated about these issues and have tried to implement realistic homework guidelines. Nonetheless, many educators still admit to overassigning homework, so several important questions remain and may be considered further as individual schools review their own policies and expectations regarding homework assignments for their students.

1. In light of what else is required during students' daily schedules, what are reasonable homework guidelines for students in grades nine through twelve?

---

[372] Kegan, *The Evolving Self*, 178.

2. Is the assigned homework truly necessary and/or intended to reinforce and enhance learning?

3. How are homework guidelines reinforced? Do students have a voice in this?*

* Some of those who participated in my research proudly reviewed the issue of recruiting students' feedback directly regarding this homework issue in the context of several other class management concerns. For example, one school revealed that they ask all their students to complete "Course Feedback" forms about *every* teacher in *every* course at the end of *every* marking period—students are allowed to complete these forms anonymously—and the first question on that form reads: "Did the teacher comply with homework guidelines?" Without a doubt, requesting students' feedback, regularly and over time, is one way of exploring and monitoring this important issue.

Beyond The Classroom

> "Tell me and I forget; teach me and I may
> remember; involve me and I learn."
> Benjamin Franklin

Many schools offer cocurricular learning experiences in a variety of programs—both on and off campus—designed to help students "to discover and develop their personal best, to seek balance in mental, physical, social and spiritual living and to make a positive difference in their communities and in the wider world."[373] In these beyond-the-classroom experiences, students (and sometimes educators, too) engage one another in a variety of fun and challenging activities that not only empower them as individuals, but also that enable them to "see" each other for who they really are beneath their academic status, physical features, ethnic identities, sexual orientations, etc. Some schools develop new-student orientation programs using these techniques, while others develop leadership training retreats for older students—juniors and seniors—as they work to nurture students' character development and a variety of leadership qualities and behaviors among their seniors and/or student-leaders. Students who participate in

---

[373] ayf.com (American Youth Foundation).

these programs usually discover much about themselves while simultaneously learning a lot about their classmates, many of whom they never would have engaged on such deep interpersonal levels. These can be very powerful encounters that not only help to break down stereotypes and foster greater tolerance but, mostly, that promote deep and mutual connections. In "fiercely competitive schools" where students, too often, are competing with each other, and where global citizenship, international mindedness, and diversity of all kinds are ever-more in demand, giving adolescents real opportunities—both in and beyond the classroom—to "find the best in themselves,"[374] to find the best in their peers, and to "value and respect those from different cultures and perspectives"[375] is certainly a developmentally empathic endeavor.

Local and Global Service Opportunities

"The best way to find yourself is to lose yourself in the service of others."
Mahatma Gandhi

Like the cocurricular learning and/or leadership training programs described above, well-designed local and global service opportunities "promote connections and understanding between people of different cultural backgrounds"[376] as "volunteers work with the people being served while learning from the experiences and views of [those] people."[377] In many ways, service experiences that take students beyond their classrooms "foster mutual respect as [students] are [temporarily] immersed in [a different] culture ... and have opportunities to learn about the history, traditions and customs of that culture." Many who participate in these service encounters report the "lasting impact"[378] of their experiences, as students return to school "with a greater awareness of others."[379] Once again, in the face of relentless competition and work demands—as well as recently increased tensions among and between various cultures, religions, and nations—even brief opportunities for students to leave school and be of service to

---

[374] Ibid.
[375] Ibid.
[376] ubuntuconnects.org.
[377] Ibid.
[378] Ibid.
[379] Ibid.

others—locally and globally—can lead to calmness and tranquility, to surprisingly different perspectives, and often, to an unanticipated sense of purpose or motivation for a new educational or career direction for those involved with the serving. In any case, in these ways, it is developmentally empathic to provide students with real opportunities to "get outside of themselves" and to experience and learn firsthand from those who are different and/or less fortunate than they are, as these experiences can be life-changing for developing—and identity searching—adolescents.

Health and Wellness Curricula

"The first wealth is health."
Ralph Waldo Emerson

Many secondary schools have already implemented structured health and wellness curricula for their students. Some schools have yearlong courses in these important topics, while others have semester-long weekly discussion groups in which health and health-related topics are reviewed in greater depth. Regardless of their curricular structures, all of these schools have recognized the preventative benefits of engaging students in these critical topics. Offering adult-guided, safe, and structured programs in which students can learn directly from and with each other provides them with opportunities to hear accurate information, to talk openly about how to integrate that information into the choices they make, and to develop trust and support from one another regarding these important—and some-times, awkward—issues. Topics such as adolescent sexuality, dating and the hookup culture, alcohol and drug awareness and relevant pressures to use, nutritional health, stress management, and knowing when and how to ask for help are just a few of the topics that most early adolescents need to learn and talk about but rarely have the safe and honest opportunities to do so.

"Best" College vs. "Best-Fit" College

"A mind is a fire to be kindled, not a vessel to be filled."
Plutarch

Deliberations about "best" colleges vs. "best-fit" colleges abound and are already the focus of many, if not most, skilled college counselors working in competitive secondary schools. One such college counselor griped that at her school, despite the advice of teachers, advisors, and even of the academic dean, parents are allowed to override the educators' placement recommendations in order to place their teenage children in the most advanced academic courses so as to enhance that student's college transcript. To my surprise—and delight, quite frankly—as this college counselor discussed this issue further with me, she stated that the most frequent question she asks of parents in these uncomfortable meetings is, *"At what cost* to [child's name] are you overriding what we think is the best course fit for [child's name], and insisting on this advanced course placement instead?" Usually, these parents are so focused on trying to get their children admitted to the "best" colleges—where they as "vessels [might] be filled" with what the "best" colleges have to offer—and are not as amenable to considering the "best-*fit*" colleges—where their children's "minds can be kindled" in sync with their actual abilities, interests, and talents. In light of how competitive the college process has become in recent years, this issue may not have been as important until now.

"A recent survey of college counseling centers has found that more than half their clients have severe psychological problems, an increase of 13 percent in just two years. Anxiety and depression, in that order, are now the most common mental health diagnoses among college students, according to the Center for Collegiate Mental Health at Penn State."[380] One of the reasons why "best fit" is so important, describes one University of Pennsylvania senior, "Nobody wants to be the one who is struggling while everyone else is doing great."[381] Further, a Penn task force that has explored and monitored these issues described how "students feel enormous pressure [because] 'a perception that one has to be perfect in every academic, co-curricular and social endeavor can manifest as demoralization, alienation or conditions like anxiety or depression.'"[382] In light of these realities, and of the "increasing suicide rate among 15- to 24-year-olds since 2007,"[383] too many of whom have been college students, striving for colleges that

---

[380] J. Scelfo, "Campus Suicide and the Pressure of Perfection," *New York Times*, July 27, 2015.
[381] Ibid.
[382] Ibid.
[383] Ibid.

are close matches between students' true abilities and interests, and what the colleges actually provide seems like a supportive strategy worth upholding. As many college counselors readily admit, there are many, many great colleges where many students would thrive, and that attending the "best" college—just because a student may be admitted—may not be the "best" college for *that* student. Too often, anxiety and depression ensue as some of these students realize that the "fit" is not as comfortable as they had anticipated.

Pressures of Diversity

"We are increasingly recognizing and accepting,
respecting and celebrating our cultural diversity."
Julie Bishop

In chapter 4, we reviewed several examples of students who had experienced "considerable and unnecessary pressure" associated with their being identified, in one way or another, as part of a minority group. Recall further that we had cited Myra McGovern of NAIS as having stated, "More independent schools are becoming invested in how diverse environments should *feel*, rather than only concentrating on what they look like."[384] Sadly, for many years prior to this, many independent schools were "largely inaccessible to minority and lower-income students,"[385] and as many of these students still acknowledge, "simply being admitted [to one of these schools] doesn't guarantee a smooth or successful educational journey."[386] Finally, as addressed most clearly by one of the educators I interviewed for this book, it doesn't matter which minority group we're talking about—racial, sexual orientation, religious affiliation, etc.—in light of how rapidly population patterns in the United States and around the world are changing, *all* schools face the ongoing adaptive challenge of creating and sustaining a truly diverse educational culture, one in which *all* students feel included, accepted, and valued for who they are as human beings. As this particular educator stated in the interview, "We need to maintain an active and

---

[384] http://www.theatlantic.com/education/archive/2013/12/when-minority-students-attend-elite-private-schools/282416/.
[385] Ibid.
[386] Ibid.

dynamic willingness to change, to make everyone feel included, and not culturally dislocated."

While many schools have already devoted considerable resources—time, money, multicultural events, and various policy changes—and are already working hard on these issues, the importance of *continuing* to strive for true diversity, in all its forms and expressions, cannot be overstated. Essentially, for *any* student who comes to a high-achieving secondary school—particularly a school that advertises itself as "an educational community that interweaves mutual respect and compassion for others with its unwavering efforts to develop students' keen and creative minds, their healthy bodies and their moral character"—to experience "considerable and unnecessary pressure" for reasons of sexual, racial, ethnic, or religious identity ... is now, and always will be, intolerable. I include this brief "supportive strategy" recommendation here in an effort to remind us all of our need to redouble our efforts to create and maintain educational *communities* that reflect true diversity ... both in what they "look like" and, mostly, "how they feel."

CHAPTER 11

We're All in This Together

One way to think about making adaptive changes within our schools is to consider that because these changes "demand innovation and learning," as we engage our multifaceted binds together, slowly but surely, *we* will adapt. Ultimately, our carefully implemented changes *will change us.* In this way, we will not just add more skills to our existing repertoire, as a mechanic or electrician might add specific skills to his or her list of repair services. Instead, we will expand the very way we know our binds; we will broaden the way we understand them, and therefore, we will change the ways we function—the ways we educate and parent our adolescents. I will attempt to unpack this process in this chapter.

The *Immunity to Change* paradigm prescribes a well-guided pathway for engaging adaptive challenges. Its approach begins with a series of careful observations of the actual effects of our "negative but widespread practices," and then follows with our cautiously but deliberately "enacting new behaviors—ones that our big assumptions would tell us not to do—in order to get information about the validity of our mindset."[387] That is, with this approach, with a thorough understanding of what we say we want—but, also, of what we actually do—the change to doing what we actually want becomes clearer. We expose the disconnect and are then better positioned to bridge it.

Before we examine the specifics of this well-guided pathway for engaging our own adaptive challenges, let's take a look at two schools—one European international school and one American independent school—both of which have already cautiously but deliberately enacted new

---

[387] Kegan and Lahey, *Immunity to Change*, 219.

behaviors in an intentional effort to empathize more with their students. That these schools are separated in geography in no way takes away from the fact that they face the same "issues" that have been detailed in this book: they are on the same track.

European International School

At this international school, a major part of the faculty's professional development occurs "in house" instead of their going only to outside workshops and professional conferences. In 2010, at the urging of one of the school's senior administrators, one member of the faculty attended an "open training" program led by National School Reform Faculty (NSRF®),[388] a training experience focused on encouraging teachers to connect more with one another, to share their best practices with each other, and, in general, to develop more coherence as a teaching faculty.

After that faculty member's initial experience in 2010, he returned to the school highly motivated to introduce a version of NSRF's Critical Friends Groups® (CFG) to other members of the faculty. Another training of ten faculty members from that same school ensued, and that group became the school's "core" group who, with support of the administrative team, began the school's first "collaborative learning community" (CLC). This initial group of ten teachers "now knew what was possible after five days of this training," said the group's leader to me. The most common areas of focus in these CLC meetings have reflected a full range of topics: questions about, or approaches to, the curriculum; reviewing and sharing instructional techniques and strategies; finding different—and frequently more creative—methods of assessment; collaborating on how to work with students who are struggling; and working on dilemmas that teachers experience as they try to work more effectively with particular students. While all this can sound like buzzwords, in fact, the work of this group has had significant impact.

Thus, strikingly, over the past six years, this in-house professional development approach has evolved to the point where, according to the original group leader, "about sixty five percent of the faculty now participate—voluntarily—in one of four existing groups of about fifteen teachers." The groups meet monthly for about two hours on school-allocated time that is dedicated to professional development. The faculty members

---

[388] http://www.nsrfharmony.org/.

who do not participate opt, instead, to do some other professional development endeavor independently ... with the approval and support of the administration.

As these groups have continued and evolved, they have fostered a deep sense of faculty cohesiveness. As one teacher said, "CLCs have brought the whole school closer together in the sense that each teacher now understands the whole school culture ... the longer-term perspective and continuity of each student's education." As teachers from different grade levels and from different subject areas work together for the common purpose of educating their students, the CLC groups help them to see "the whole student ... over time" more effectively. Specifically, they understand more about their students as they enter the school, as they progress through the different grade levels and subject areas, and finally, how they present—with capacities they both have and have not developed—as they prepare to graduate. As this group leader stated further, "As a faculty, we've become a conscious culture that thinks about how people communicate ... about how we listen to each other, and for me, that's probably the biggest change ... and I think many of my colleagues would say the same thing. It's increasingly about how we address each other, how we listen to each other ... so how else do you build empathy, right?"

As I neared the end of my interview with one of the CLC group leaders, I asked, "Now that you've implemented these groups and have been developing them for the past six years, has this approach to professional development changed your minds somehow? Can you imagine returning to 'the old way of doing things' wherein these CLC groups were not part of your work environment?"

To my question, this group leader said, "For the teachers, particularly those who have invested in this process for more than one or two years, it has definitely changed their minds. The CLCs put people in a collaborative space to share their work ... in a space where they feel safe to put something out there that's not perfect ... or to put out a need they might have ... and I would say for those people, it has absolutely changed their minds." Another group leader stated, "The CLCs are a thriving and vital part of professional growth at our school and their impact has gone beyond the dedicated CLC time. As one of our trained coaches has said, 'there is a cross-pollination of both ideas and the tools that are used and they have impacted faculty meetings, small groups and classroom teaching.'"[389]

---

[389] NSRF ® "*Connections*," 15.

Reportedly, the administrators have changed their minds, too, I was told, because, as one of the group leaders said, "They see it ... they work with this group of teachers who are more connected with each other, who are more committed to their work, to their profession as teachers ... and to this school." Finally, one of the CLC group leaders acknowledged, "Our willingness to be transparent, open and responsive has been key to building trust both with our membership and with the administrative team. We are fortunate that our administration has realized that just as teachers need to change their role in the classroom to become facilitators of their students' learning, administrators, too, need to take that leap of faith to become facilitators (rather than directors) of teachers continuing professional growth."[390]

As you can well imagine, these ongoing and collaborative faculty work groups encourage teachers to share deeply with one another. In fact, they share not only their achievements and successes, but also, their needs, errors, and failures. In this way, these teachers share more deeply of themselves, of who they are. As they strive together in the context of these safe and trusting groups, these teachers grow and develop together—and *that* is the power of their in-house professional development. Furthermore, because of this shared growth and development among the teachers, their students benefit, too. In a related way, one of my close friends and colleagues, Dr. Harry Parad, has often said, "When the key adults in students' lives are on the same page, students can't help but learn and grow in the direction of the adults' coordinated communication." With respect to this international school, without a doubt, the students there are taught by energized, respectful, and highly intentional teachers who are increasingly "coordinated" in their teaching efforts. Because of that purposeful adult coordination, students experience their teachers not only as "coordinated," but as remarkably caring and focused on them, as genuine and authentic—and as a cohesive group of faculty members, which benefits the school itself. Because of these "intangibles," the students feel understood and recognized for who they are, and, therefore, they are more motivated to produce higher-quality work within such a respectful, intentional, and empathic school. As this group leader shared with me at the end of our interview, "Overall, we started these groups because we wanted to create a space where faculty could directly dive deeper into their work with students and to share ways to improve how we reach all of them."

---

[390] Ibid.

American Independent School

Consider another school's decision to move away from a traditional schedule of eight forty- or fifty-minute periods that met every day, to adopt a block schedule, one that consists of longer class periods that meet fewer times each week. While there are, indeed, various pros and cons regarding block scheduling, one of its benefits is that within block scheduling, students tend to have less homework every night as they prepare for fewer class meetings for each day. Importantly, during the year before actually electing to make this change, this school organized a "task force" comprising several classroom teachers and some administrators. This task force met regularly, over time, to consider and discuss the various pros and cons they had heard about block scheduling. In addition, the school invited "a few talking heads"—outside professionals who were already experienced with block scheduling—to visit and speak at a few faculty meetings, as these individuals could provide more details regarding the advantages and disadvantages of block scheduling. At the end of this careful process, as one of the administrators of this school reported, "We did this, primarily, to minimize transitions during the school day, and to reduce the stress on students by not requiring homework in every class every night ... because we learned that within block scheduling, homework assignments tend to be more spread out." In a traditional eight-period school day, "students must prepare for more courses, which can be overwhelming and have an adverse impact on learning."[391] This administrator continued, "Now that we've had this schedule for so long, we have learned that it offers students more flexibility for pursuing their interests. For example, as it occurs rather frequently, class discussions often get going and our longer class periods enable the students and teacher to get into them in greater depth."

In this school, after more than a decade of implementation, most courses meet three times weekly: twice for eighty minutes and once for forty-five minutes. This schedule gives faculty members the flexibility to incorporate a broad range of academic tools—such as labs and technology, and, sometimes, local field trips. Perhaps most importantly, "Our intentional pacing offers students a less hurried everyday schedule."

When I asked about whether there had been resistance to moving to block scheduling fifteen years ago, this administrator stated, "Yes,

---

[391] http://edglossary.org/block-schedule/.

primarily from teachers who were already used to teaching their 45-50 minute classes, and also from some teachers who wanted more repetition and more frequent class meetings to more regularly reinforce rote learning, especially in foreign languages and lower-level math courses. These teachers certainly had a good point, but in our fifteen years of using this schedule, most of those teachers have adjusted their approaches."

When I asked about how block scheduling met their initial goal of trying to be more "empathic" with their students, this administrator responded by stating, "Block scheduling introduces more variability (which we think is a good thing for adolescents), more opportunities to explore ideas deeply … often at the will of the students … and it gives equal time to visual and performing arts as it does to math, science, and the humanities. In many schools, math, science, and humanities tend to dominate the schedule, and too often, the arts take a backseat to the more 'academically rigorous' subjects. At this school, we believe in fostering students' creativity as much as we foster their academic abilities. To us, this is empathic because it's a more balanced schedule that emphasizes the 'whole child,' not just the academic child."

Finally, just as when I asked this same question of the European international school CLC group leader, about whether it was possible to imagine returning to the "before," I asked this independent school administrator: "Now that you've implemented block scheduling and have been working with it for the past fifteen years, has this approach to scheduling changed your minds somehow? Can you imagine returning to 'the old way of doing things,' to the traditional eight-period school day?" Without a second thought, this administrator stated, "There is no doubt that block scheduling has changed our minds about scheduling. In fact, at this point, if we announced that we were planning to go back to the traditional eight-period school day schedule, we'd have a war on our hands. Both the faculty and the students would be asking us, 'Are you insane?'"

What Can We Learn from These Schools?

It is worth noting that both of these examples reflect decisions that emerged organically—from within these schools themselves. Further, and most important, both decisions led both schools to new ways of seeing things, to new ways of knowing themselves as educators, and ultimately, to new ways of operating within their schools that reflect the kinds of things schools should be considering in order to be more empathic with their students. That is, what they ultimately enacted not only was triggered by a concern for students, but ended up beneficial to them, enacted institutionally.

Further, what stands out about both these schools' change processes is how "cohesive" they became before they became more developmentally empathic for their students. In both examples, and by very different approaches, the faculty members and the administrators worked together—they engaged adaptive change processes—and those deliberate and thoughtful interactions, over time, led one school to become "a more conscious culture that thinks about how people communicate," and another school to come to a shared consensus—another form of cohesiveness—as they took measures, "primarily, to minimize transitions during the school day, and to reduce the stress on students by not requiring homework in every class every night."

In both examples, "becoming cohesive" was, itself, a developmental process in which the adults committed to working together to make adaptive changes, engaging openly with one another, and sometimes, struggling together—and that very process led to their new and different ways of knowing not only the challenges they were facing, but also, to new and different ways of knowing each other and themselves. Ironically, these very different approaches to problem solving resulted in a very similar outcome: adaptation, characterized by a deeper group cohesiveness, also known as group "development." As a result of this deep and shared development, both groups were then better positioned to make riskier changes—and to deal more effectively ("more cohesively") with the consequences.

Finally, by mentioning these two examples, I do *not* mean to suggest that all schools should engage intentional professional development faculty groups, or that they should rush to adopt block scheduling. Instead, I mention these two examples as a way of revealing how individual schools can and often do make developmentally empathic changes. As we discussed in chapter 10, there is not one list of specific changes that all schools should make, as all schools vary in their curricular structures and in their overall approaches to their work. What is most important, however, is that whatever changes individual schools decide to make—and however they decide to make them—they need to maintain a central focus on "developmental empathy" for their students first, as *that* is what is needed most *now* in these ultracompetitive and high-achieving environments. As we have discussed throughout this book, for too long, competitive and high-achieving schools have focused too much on an "only the best will do" mind-set, and that mind-set has led to the harm and detriment of too many students whose natural developmental capacities are simply not ready to maintain an "only the best will do" approach for the balance of their daily lives.

In each of these examples, as the schools enacted new behaviors, based on new ideas about what would be possible to do, and then gathered information and feedback about how these new behaviors were working out, they both came to new insights, to new ways of knowing—to new mind-sets. Essentially, because of these courageous decisions to try new actions that led to resulting changes—changes that their previous assumptions suggested were almost unthinkable—both schools gradually but effectively "changed their minds." Now, with new information that has come from their own lived and carefully considered experience, both schools cannot imagine returning to the old or "traditional" ways of doing things. These "mind-changing" actions and resulting behavioral changes have constituted a win-win for both schools. While the educators (faculty members and administrators) have developed unexpected "growth mindsets,"[392] the students have also benefitted by having more "grown and developed" teachers—more insightful, more authentic, more empathic—who, because of their *own* growth and development, have motivated their students to work hard within a carefully considered and carefully presented curriculum.

We might even be able to say that the educators in these two schools have found ways to realize their primary and fundamental commitments—the very ones they identified, and that we reviewed in chapter 2. Recall that educators from nearly all the schools I interviewed stated their fundamental commitments "to presenting our students with an appropriate balance of challenge and support; to authentic engagement with our students; to educating our students in healthy, safe and balanced ways; to facilitating students' positive self-exploration and growth; to promoting a healthy school culture; and perhaps most of all, to meeting our students where they are."

What Happened

Having examined these two schools' intentional approaches to becoming more developmentally empathic, we now return to the *Immunity to Change*'s

---

[392] C. S. Dweck, *Mindset: The New Psychology of Success* (New York, Ballantine Books, 2006).

"well guided pathway for engaging our adaptive challenges." Just as the European international school and the American independent school made deliberate decisions to test their previous assumptions, we need to test our assumptions, too. For, in fact, over the years these assumptions have neither been challenged nor tested. At the outset, at the international school, the administrators acknowledged feeling suspicious, maybe a little threatened, about allowing collaborative learning communities. For the independent school, the faculty and administrators initially considered it risky to leave the safety and predictability of their traditional eight-period schedule to try block scheduling. As we saw, after their own careful processes, both schools enacted new ways of operating to see if their assumptions were actually true. The fact that both schools embraced the changes is evidence that they both grew and developed to make the changes happen. They expanded their ways knowing, of accepting possibilities and creating ways for these to be initiated, such that they now operate within the newfound safety born of their new ways of operating. These changes now reflect the "organizational culture"[393] of these schools, also known as "The way we do things around here!"

Recall some of the assumptions we reviewed in chapter 2. Many educators stated assumptions such as, "If we didn't overschedule our students and assign so much work, then we would be seen as having lost our standards and lacking in rigor and excellence." Another educator stated his assumption, "If we didn't overschedule our students, assign so much homework and over-focus on the college process, then we would be perceived as intellectually soft, and our students wouldn't get into selective colleges." Finally, one administrator admitted to assuming, "If we actually gave in, and a developmentally reasonable schedule emerged, we might achieve a healthy balance for our students at the cost of our school's distinctiveness; we might lose our edge of excellence and become a vanilla school, and who would want to come to a vanilla school?"

To be sure, just beginning to test these assumptions by enacting new behaviors, with the accompanying changes that our previous assumptions would tell us not to do ... is very tricky business. Quite frankly, even considering the possibility of enacting new behaviors that challenge our basic assumptions is sure to elicit some anxiety because it does, indeed, feel risky to jump into these potentially dangerous waters—where, because our assumptions are challenged, our behaviors must accommodate.

---

[393] http://www.businessdictionary.com/definition/organizational-culture.html.

Nonetheless, this testing phase is critical for the longer-term process of implementing real and lasting changes. As Kegan and Lahey state, "Our immediate purpose [in generating relevant tests of our assumptions] is not to improve or get better, but just to get information,"[394] information that will help us to make more carefully considered but still-deliberate changes over time. Essentially, during this testing phase—which can take several months or even a few years—"we are working within the sweet spot of an adaptive challenge, discovering whether it is possible to replace the safety born of limiting ourselves [to the old ways of operating] with the safety informed by learning that the expected bad outcomes [from new ways of operating] don't materialize when we suspend self-imposed limits."[395]

Without this testing phase, we risk adopting "quick fix" changes too swiftly, only to see them backfire and result in our abandoning them when the anxiety they would surely provoke would begin to emerge. The actions initiated within these change endeavors must take into account the feelings and the behavioral responses triggered by those changes. At a minimum, the anxieties that are often associated with even the idea of taking steps to make changes must be considered related to the specific change envisioned.

This testing phase, thus, reflects a series of cautious but deliberate steps to prevent us from revisiting our anxieties, and to keep us from reactivating our collective immunities to changing. As Kegan and Lahey remind us, "Intentional action, data collection, and interpreting the data are the core means we use to mine the gap between our intentions and our current ability to deliver on them."[396]

A Pathway to Change

The *Immunity to Change* paradigm, which I have been utilizing throughout this book, suggests that after a progression of making these cautious but deliberate changes in which we incorporate feedback from our collective testing efforts—and then revise our assumptions accordingly—we can and will adapt. The changes we "cautiously and deliberately" make will help us to adapt, or as mentioned at the start of this chapter, "our changes will change us." Like the educators described in the two examples mentioned above, we

---

[394] Kegan and Lahey, *Immunity to Change*, 220.
[395] Ibid.
[396] Ibid.

will grow and develop as we intentionally expand the very ways in which we know and understand our binds. Moreover, from this newly developed perspective, we will be able to more safely adjust our behavior—without the anxieties that have burdened us to date—to reflect the various ways in which we will have grown. This cautious but deliberate growth process directed at changes within our institutions **for our students**—itself a gradual evolution of who *we* are, and, therefore, of how *we* educate and parent our kids—urges our corrective thinking and behavior while it simultaneously respects our fears and anxieties. Mostly, this cautious but deliberate growth process reflects a truly developmental stance, one that Kegan and Lahey claim to be "at the heart of individual and collective change."[397]

Do you recognize the powerful irony here? Paradoxically, in our collective efforts to reverse our established practices of not truly respecting our students' developmental capacities, we—the adults—will have begun to respect and appreciate our own. As shown in the two examples above, as we work together—challenging and supporting one another—working to find ways to enable our students to learn and grow in healthy, safe, and balanced ways within the boundaries of their true developmental capacities, *we* will learn and grow, too. That developmental stance signifies the essence of overcoming the immunity to change, and of what is actually possible while striving together for adaptive solutions. In the end, the "innovation and learning" that we will experience as a result of our collective and cooperative efforts will reflect our previously unimagined adaptation, our own growth and development.

Who would have guessed that transforming our schools would necessitate that we focus first on transforming ourselves? Ironically, that means growth and development for *us*—educators and parents—in environments that are overtly focused on the growth and development of students. Essentially, the more *we* grow, the better *we* will be at creating and sustaining developmentally empathic schools for our students. Remember: "We are responsible for the cultures we create." If we remain stagnant, however, if we refuse to change and grow, then we need to be willing to ask ourselves, "At what cost" … to our students, to our schools and to ourselves … are we actually inclined to make this decision?

---

[397] Ibid., 308.

ABOUT THE AUTHOR

David Gleason, Psy.D., is a clinical psychologist specializing in counseling and evaluating students in competitive schools throughout the United States, Europe, and Asia. He is the founder and director of Developmental Empathy LLC, a consulting group engaged in helping schools make "developmentally empathic" changes for students while maintaining academic excellence. He regularly speaks at schools and international conferences on ameliorating the conditions described in *At What Cost?*

Made in the USA
Lexington, KY
17 September 2017